Friends in Low Places

Radcliffe Medical Press

Radcliffe Medical Press Ltd
18 Marcham Road, Abingdon, Oxon OX14 1AA

British Library Cataloguing in Publication Data

A catalogue record for this book is available from the British Library.

ISBN 1 85775 404 2

Typeset by Aarontype Limited, Easton, Bristol
Printed and bound by TJ International Ltd, Padstow, Cornwall

Contents

Foreword

Once upon a time when the world was young and I was editor of *World Medicine* many of the unsolicited manuscripts I received were quietly interred in a file labelled 'Whither the future?'. A fair share were written by GPs of a certain age who after years of happily plying their craft realised that they couldn't define exactly what they were doing. In search of understanding they donned the robes of poet or philosopher and, for a moment, raised their eyes towards the stars. Sadly, most chose to do so on a cloudy night so their interpretations of the mysteries of their craft were misted o'er with what Sir Peter Medawar used to call 'analgesic explanation' which dulls the ache of incomprehension without removing the cause.

James Willis has avoided this trap. His observations are what you would expect from a GP who keeps his eyes, his ears and his imagination open but there's nothing analgesic – or ethereal – about his ideas for they all derive from his daily experience here on earth. One of the delights of this book is that the further you read into it the more its message becomes indistinguishable from the messenger. Just as his life as a GP mingles inextricably with those of his patients, so his thinking merges inextricably with his activities as father, writer, amateur singer, sailor, versifier, tennis player, theatregoer, teacher's husband and dedicated argumentator.

What we hear is a distinctive voice – an individual sound that reconfirms one of the messages of this book that those who labour in low places, who take account of relative values and feelings in their judgements, acquire a wisdom denied to those in high places who search eagerly for computable 'evidence' to help them protect 'people out there'. (A defining characteristic of those in high places is their habit of referring to the admass that inhabits the middle ground twixt high people, the policy makers and low people, the doers, as 'people out there'.)

GPs will find this book cathartic. A crescendo of assenting growls will be heard across the land when they reach the chapters on managerialism and the Utopian protocols created in a world where every activity has to be evidence based – except of course NHS management.

Yet the folk in high places are not villains. Most are intelligent, well-meaning people who seek to do their best, their decisions conditioned by the filtered information they receive. The filters are built into the system. Politicians tend to appoint 'advisers' who agree with what they've already decided to do; and, though focus groups can be a useful way of assessing ideas that already exist, they are a hopeless way of creating new ones.

It's not only in politics that selectivity is part of the process. When I was a member of the GMC I was condemned to read interminable accounts of doctors mistreating their patients. Disturbing though it was to learn what a few calculating wrongdoers had got away with, even more dispiriting were the tales of shambling incompetence, of doctors who didn't really care, who had no insight into their inadequacies, no interest in doing their job well, just in getting it done. I had to keep reminding myself that this was a highly selective view of medicine and sought to exorcise it by going as often as I could to postgraduate meetings where enthusiasts discussed ways of improving their skills.

It's not only high places that offer distorted views. Those who inhabit lower ground need to recognise that not all their problems are imposed from above. GPs certainly need the wisdom that James Willis ascribes to them but they also need knowledge. And there are signs of a dangerous dearth of knowledge – or, at least of its application – in some low-lying areas. When a newspaper sent simulated patients to a small number of GPs in London and Manchester, half the doctors were happy to offer beta-blockers to a man with asthma and allow a woman with classical migraine to take the combined contraceptive pill.

Seen from on high these look like dangerous acts committed by incompetent individuals, yet Phil Hammond, a medical commentator not renowned for pulling his punches, offered a more complex explanation:

GPs are under enormous time pressure (most of the consultations were at least half an hour late) and many suffer from stress, depression and burn-out. Even more (myself included) find it increasingly difficult to empathise with patients, address their concerns and remember all the questions we should ask to prescribe safely – all in the space of six minutes. My guess is that if I phoned all these doctors and asked them if you should give beta-blockers to a patient with asthma, or the Pill to a woman with a migraine with an aura, they would say 'no'. Yet translating this basic knowledge into the stress of every day practice is a lot harder.

GPs have to do the translating for themselves. Like James Willis, I'm persuaded by my own experience that it can't be enforced by managerial diktat that seeks to impose perfection on an imperfect world. When I left medicine and ventured into the market place I discovered that the organisations in which I worked most productively and most happily were those in which management was a background activity that intruded on our daily lives only as a butt for complaint if we felt disgruntled. Administrators in those companies practised a sophisticated art. Unlike the administrators in less successful enterprises in which I laboured, they judged our value by what we produced not by checking the times we clocked in or clocked out, nor by counting the hours we sat at our desks gazing out the window and longing for our watches to signal the time to go home.

Then in the 1990s something nasty happened. Two national institutions for which I'd worked – both rather special, maybe because they were created by people who cared – fell victim to the same destructive process. Egged on by politicians eager to centralise power, people in high places in the BBC and the NHS decided that management consultants and focus groups were a more reliable source of wisdom than those who made programmes or looked after patients. As happens when control becomes centralised, management by diktat had an irresistible appeal to the new controllers. Compelled to make 'arm's length' decisions, they devised their strategies on models constructed from the evidence with which they'd been provided.

Their models had – indeed still have – two serious flaws: first, the only evidence they recognise is the sort that can be manipulated in a spreadsheet and, second, much of that 'hard evidence' has a soft centre. One of life's ironies, neatly illustrated on pages 126–7, is that a lot of it derives from the activities of those whom the diktators seek to manage and who know much better than their masters how corrupt the data are.

This book offers a different way of seeking solutions. Planners and administrators, it argues, need to acknowledge how great is the divide between their most sophisticated models and the reality 'out there' and thus recognise that the most valuable evidence on offer from those in low places is the evidence of their daily experience.

With that I agree. I cannot, however, accept James Willis' complaint that his friends in low places remain unheard. Read on and you will discover that they have found a persuasive voice.

Michael O'Donnell
November 2000

About the author

James Willis has been a general practitioner in a small, personal practice in Alton, Hampshire for 28 years. Since the success of his first book, *The Paradox of Progress*, he has been a regular contributor and columnist in the medical press.

Acknowledgements

For more than three years I have been discussing the material in this book with almost everybody I have met. Their generosity, imagination and patience are beyond praise, if not beyond belief. To mention them all would be impossible and any attempt to do so would risk the grave unfairness of omission. Many of them I have named in the text or in the references; only the names and identifying details of patients have been changed.

However, I must record my special thanks to Martyn Evans and David Greaves, who set me on course at a personal tutorial in Swansea; to Steve Vincent, who finally got my study leave application approved; to Michael O'Donnell, of course; Bruce Charlton, Iona Heath, Jeremy Harvey and Desmond Rissik, who read drafts and gave me fearless feedback and wonderful support; and to my partner, Philip Hopwood, who willingly ran the practice during my absence, making the whole thing possible. It has been a joy to work again with Radcliffe Medical Press, and with Jamie Etherington my editor.

My final thanks must go to all the people with whom, in countless conversations, in my surgery, in their homes, on walks, in bars, on holidays, I have developed my ideas. They know who they are and it is to them, almost needless to say, that I dedicate this book:

To my friends in low places.

Professional people . . . are under siege – they are caught between power-ful opposing forces. On the one hand they see a world demanding greater value for money and accountability, where their autonomy is threatened, and their professional actions are being brought under control. On the other hand they know intuitively that professional people need autonomy, that professionalism is hugely complex, that being a professional is so much more than the acquisition of certain skills or a set of competencies. Yet they are aware too that they cannot easily explain the need for this autonomy, why they require such a lengthy education, and why they should be trusted.

Della Fish and Colin Coles[1]

CHAPTER ONE

They'll want you to
measure something . . .

All that twaddle . . . I mean, if you drop a patient knowing that you had
a weak knee, the patient can sue **you.**

A patient explaining why she is giving up nursing

Everyone wants to know what I am doing with my six months off.

'Is it true you are writing a book?'

I start to explain, 'I'm interested in the interface between human values and technological progress . . .' and immediately sense the familiar flash of regret that the question has been asked. I see the listener's face adopting an expression of friendly interest, bracing for a long ride, but my enthusiasm keeps me going:

'All these rules and regulations that we are producing all the time, making everything better and better and safer and safer, are taking the *humanity* out of life, turning everybody into machines, driving us all mad . . .'

As a GP you have to be sensitive to people, and suddenly I know that the interest is genuine. People within earshot turn and start to listen. I have struck the familiar chord: 'Yes . . . yes . . . , that sounds really interesting . . . , that is *so* true . . .'

'All the time in our daily lives we find ourselves having to comply with official stipulations which seem like madness. At the same time we all know that there is another perspective from which these crazy rules make sense. I really believe that the people holding both views are good, honourable people, doing what they sincerely believe to be right. So I want to know how on earth these utterly different views of the same issues can be reconciled.'

Again there are enthusiastic nods of agreement. I give an example: 'Several of my wife's teaching colleagues attended a first-aid course last term at which they were told that they must not apply antiseptic, they must not remove splinters, and that if a child needs a plaster for a cut they must be made to put it on themselves. A few days after the course certificates of competence arrived in the post for each of them. These were all experienced teachers who had brought up their own families and who regularly took parties of schoolchildren on trips abroad. The effect of the course was almost entirely to deskill them, but they got their certificates.'

During the last few weeks before I came away, patients leaving through the surgery door kept turning back to ask me the same question, 'What are you writing about?', and I gave them the same sort of reply. And their reaction was always the same. They knew exactly what I meant. Several of them said, 'Well, you've got a best-seller there.'

It had not been so easy to persuade the National Health Service Executive that what I was planning for my sabbatical was worthwhile.[2] They wanted me to say what I was going to find before I started looking, which was rather a fundamental problem. They thought 'focus' was essential for my project, whereas one of the things that I wanted my project to be about was the validity of work that is *not* focused. Anyway, I tried for five years to get approval, while others seemed to be having no difficulty.

'They'll want you to measure something,'[3] said David Morrell sadly, soon after I had been turned down for the second time. Years earlier, during my student elective in general practice, he had been a lecturer in the university practice I visited in Edinburgh. I had accompanied him on foot on visits, watching him sink his daunting height into the deepest chairs available, witnessing the way he was welcomed, respected and trusted. This experience was a substantial part of my inspiration to become a GP.[4]

It was years – almost a whole career – before we met again, during which time he became Professor of General Practice and then President of the British Medical Association. I had been fond of telling people that I knew he was a *real* GP. But now when I asked his advice he also knew the score. 'They' would want me to 'measure something' – and he knew how difficult it would be to change them.

To his credit, however, he did not share the general view that there was an easy answer to my problem. So many other people kept telling me that I should dream up some plausible-sounding project (it didn't matter what), send in my protocol, acceptance would be automatic, and then (conspiratorial wink) I could do what I liked. 'You just have to play the game', was what they always said.

Nothing can possibly go wrong . . .

It makes you feel old-fashioned, having scruples about this sort of thing, but the feeling is becoming a familiar one. According to the new, official model, people like me are *history*.[5] The days when a doctor could act on his own, weigh up a situation on its merits, make a judgement, exhibit flair and individuality, and *make mistakes*, are behind us. It was fun at the time, but we have moved beyond that – the world can no longer afford real people like that. In future we must become rule-followers like everybody else, and it will all work out better that way. It won't all happen immediately, of course, as the details will take a while to perfect, but ultimately that is the way it will be.

However, I keep remembering the old joke about the passengers on an aircraft and the in-flight announcement: 'We are happy to inform you that you have just taken off in the world's first fully-automatic aircraft. There are no crew of any kind on board. Just relax and enjoy your flight. Nothing can possibly go wrong . . . go wrong . . . go wrong . . . go wrong . . .'

That's it, really – the central question. It is the crux of the whole thing. Are 'they', 'we' or whoever really going to get it right in the end, so that 'nothing can possibly go wrong'? Are we going to get the whole thing encoded in an all-encompassing computer program which has the answer to everything? Or is that a dream which is inherently impossible and which will elude us forever, however clever we become and however sophisticated our systems and our machines may be? So that we will need the human abilities of people forever?

Not just the 'why', but also the 'how'

I believe the latter. I also believe that it doesn't really matter that I also *hope* the latter because, if so, that would leave a space and a purpose for you and me. What we are talking about here is the best way of organising a modern society – it isn't going to be enough just to organise it so that GPs, teachers and people like us can continue to have a rewarding and satisfying life. That could be used as a justification for maintaining a thousand obsolete niches, from scribes and court-jesters to the bangers of the timing-drums on the slave galleys in the film *Ben Hur*.

However, if on the other hand there is a role for the qualities of the individual human mind in the functioning of our society which is *essential*, and which will always continue to be essential, then that is something entirely different. It would mean that human abilities are not just the 'why' of life, but that they are also the 'how'. It would mean that for society to turn its back on human abilities would be nothing short of madness.

CHAPTER TWO

Surrounded by the 'madness'

'Ropey old junk you gave me. You know what you read about antibiotics in the papers, what will all this rubbish be doing to my system?'

'Well, in the good old days before antibiotics you'd probably have died of a leg like that' (solemn thumbs down).

'What? Are you serious?'

'Either that or you'd have had your leg amputated.'

Sir,

As the husband of a primary school teacher and parent of three children passing through the maintained education system, I should like to respond to Mr Woodhead's remarks ('Why testing is no enemy of children's creativity', 20 July).

I have reluctantly reached the conclusion that in the primary sector the so-called culture of accountability has begun to go much too far.

In my wife's small six-teacher school there is now imposed a detailed and prescriptive eight-tiered planning system (yearly, termly, half-termly, weekly, daily, literacy hour, numeracy hour, and plans for individual pupils), the format of which constantly changes, and which takes each teacher many hours per week to complete.

The effects of virtually every area of school activity have now been monitored, recorded and 'evidenced'.

In the autumn my wife's school will undergo its third inspection in six years.

We need to be asking at what point it all begins to become counter-productive. That point has long been passed in the primary school sector. The planning and inspection regime seems to be wholly disproportionate.

It is hardly surprising that teachers who are in a position to do so, my wife among them, are beginning to think seriously about leaving the profession.

J M Baten
Dorchester, Dorset
Independent letters, 26 July 1999

Inner relief

Alton must be one of the smallest towns in the UK to have an *inner* relief road, but it has and we are proud of it, and this morning it is locked solid with jammed traffic. This is going to make me late for surgery because, despite my good intentions, I almost always allow myself just the four minutes my journey to work normally takes. Today it is taking me 15 minutes, and at least one of my patients will be waiting. A *patient* patient, I hope . . .

When I eventually reach the cause of the hold-up, a few yards short of the Health Centre, it turns out to be a set of temporary traffic lights for some road works. And they are obviously not even necessary. All of the workmen's equipment is well off the carriageway, and the cordons enclose nothing but the generous amount of empty road that is required by new regulations designed to protect road workers. This morning, however, the road workers are in no danger at all, because they are not there yet. Their equipment is still covered up for the night. So they cannot see for themselves what their failure to apply common sense has done to what passes for Alton's fuming rush-hour.

Have you *read* what they do?

I park the car and head straight into surgery. I apologise to Mrs Fennel, who has been waiting to talk about her dementing father.

'Don't worry, doctor', she says, 'I know how busy you are'. I apologise to Miss X who has an infected toe, and Mr Y who has a harmless mole on his back. I am still running late when I get to Mrs Borage.

Mrs Borage comes in looking agitated and angry. Nothing to do with the wait, though – she has brought back the new blood-pressure tablets I gave her last week. She is waving the packet.

'So what do you think of them?'

'I haven't even taken them.' Her pent-up indignation explodes: 'Have you read what they do? Have you *read* what they do?'

I know the problem extremely well. She has been reading the warning sheet in the packaging, which gives a complete list of every side-effect that has ever been suspected for the medicine I'm trying to persuade her to take, including some unpleasant-sounding ways of dying. They are all extraordinarily rare, of course, modern medicines being the safest and most effective in the history of the world, and certainly enormously rarer than the side-effects of *not* taking the treatment – not mentioned in the sheet – which also include some unpleasant ways of dying.

It is not at all uncommon to have several patients a day coming to surgery just for this reason – because they have been frightened by a warning sheet. We have a code on our practice computer system which means 'Patient worried by drug safety insert', and it is one of the commoner reasons for consultations. Indeed, this isn't so much a 'side-effect' of warning sheets, as their *main* effect. It represents a huge use of time and a huge amount of aggravation. Not that this appears to be of any concern to the drug companies, who merely say that they are 'covering themselves' – which makes me think of Adam and Eve and fig leaves.

Anyway, I've been Mrs Borage's doctor for 25 years, and that seems to have led her to doubt that I am deliberately poisoning her, which is nice, but has left her with the alternative conclusion that I am dangerously ignorant. Hence the red face and the angry shaking of the insert slip that I have so obviously failed to read.

And she is still waiting for the answer to her question, 'Have you *read* what they do?'

And, actually, yes, I *have* read what ACE inhibitors do. And, actually, yes, I *told* her what they do when I gave her the prescription – for example, the important point about some people occasionally fainting after the first dose. Not that it has yet happened to a patient of mine, but it is certainly common enough to mention. Something like, 'Don't walk along the edge of a cliff an hour after taking the first dose.' I also mentioned the very common ACE-inhibitor cough. But I didn't place much emphasis on the bits about dying, simply because Mrs Borage was far more likely to die if she didn't have the treatment, that being the whole point of what I was trying to do. She was certainly far more likely to have a stroke, which some people think can be worse than dying.

She and I have been agonising for months about whether or not to treat her blood pressure, because everything she has tried so far has given her side-effects. The root of the problem is that she absolutely hates the thought of taking any 'drugs' at all – a view with which, as it happens, I have a great deal of sympathy. Treating blood pressure is one of the least satisfying activities in the whole of medicine, turning people who feel well and have no idea that there is anything 'wrong' with them into lifelong tablet-takers who often experience side-effects of one type or another. The whole point about ACE inhibitors is that, despite their enormous cost, they have *fewer* side-effects than other treatments – for example, they are much less likely to make men impotent, which is no trivial consideration.

Anyway, I launch into my tutorial on drug warning sheets, opening with a line borrowed from my partner: 'The thing you have to understand about the warnings in drug packets is that they are there to protect the manufacturer, not to help you.'

Mrs Borage nods, seeing the point at once, and I continue, 'Modern drugs are used by literally millions of people all over the world, and if there is just one report of a serious reaction, even if there is no evidence that it is connected, the manufacturer will have to put it on the list, otherwise anyone else who gets the same problem will be able to sue them in a blaze of publicity because they weren't warned.'

And so, struggling to control my own blood pressure, I return for the umpteenth time to explaining why I must control *hers* . . .

It was so much simpler in the old days. Predecessors just said things like, 'Good God, you only just got to me in time – start taking these tablets straight away.' There was no nonsense about telling them the name, or anything about the drug being prescribed. The bottle would simply be labelled 'the tablets', and anyone who had the temerity to ask the pharmacist what they were would be grandly told, 'That is a matter between your doctor and me.'[6] And in those days tablets really *were* dangerous. Reserpine, for example, which was widely used to treat blood pressure at the time when I started in practice, was associated with countless (because of course in those days they remained uncounted) suicides.[7]

'Do you know,' I say at last, returning my thoughts to the gritty reality of *fin de siècle* medicine and Mrs Borage, 'if I leave your blood pressure as it is and you have a stroke, you would have a legal case against me – for not looking after you properly.'

She sits up primly, genuinely shocked, 'Oh, I wouldn't sue you . . .'

At last she decides to give the tablets a try.[8]

'Steroids'

On we go with a cough. Then Mrs Clove with a rash on her stomach which was eagerly pointed out by her three-year-old daughter.

'Have you got a rash like Mummy, Rosie?'

'No, I've got *nits*.'

Then a man who is ready to go back to work after a prostate operation. Then we've got another one:

Mr Chicory, aged 74 years, has come for review a week after I started him on prednisolone – '*steroids*' – for polymyalgia rheumatica. The history was typical from the start – crippling muscular aches and morning stiffness. His ESR[9] was very high at 78 mm/hour. I was pretty confident of the diagnosis, but his appearance in the waiting-room as I go to fetch him now is the clincher (I go and get my patients these days, instead of pressing my buzzer, partly to postpone my own seizing-up process). The way he jumps up, grinning brightly, and follows me briskly settles the issue. Better, he says, within six hours of taking the first dose.

'50% better?'

'Oh, more than 50%. More like 90%. Mind you,' . . . here we go, wait for it . . . 'the chemist was worried by the tablets you gave me.'

Yes, here's the warning sheet ready in his hand, being waved at me with a freedom of movement not experienced for many months, 'The chemist took me on one side and told me these "*steroids*" could thin my bones and do all sorts of things. He said to make sure I showed you this sheet.'

This is really too much. He can now walk freely, get out of bed, light the fire, boil a kettle – all for the first time in ages. The sort of transformation, in fact, that in a less enlightened age people would have called a miracle.

'Were you put off by the chemist?'

'Yes, I was, very put off. I nearly didn't take them.'

As he goes out I am fuming again. I flag the notes to remind me to dictate a letter to the pharmacist, to point out that I have been treating polymyalgia rheumatica with steroids for a quarter of a century, and that I am already aware that there are certain snags. Would he please support me in encouraging Mr Chicory to go on taking the tablets if, as is likely, he will have to continue on a small dose for several years until the illness burns itself out. I will, as always, be glad of suggestions for better treatments, but would he please try to make them to me and not directly to the patient . . .

Something about teaching . . .

On with an earache, then someone with hayfever and piles, who has also got a question about his aunt in Gloucester, an old man who has been coughing blood, a crying baby (I mean the baby's crying is the problem), and now Mrs Thyme is here for her HRT[10] check.

It is a sign that I am growing up that a lot of the women who used to come to me for pills to stop them getting pregnant are now coming to me for pills to stop them getting hot flushes. Mrs Thyme has the sort of blurred-at-the-edges look about her which is characteristic of the extremely over-wrought teacher. Doctors generally agree that there is something about teaching, and that it is getting worse.

She tells me that she has just worked out that she has to complete 800 extra forms per year compared to six years ago when she started teaching. She was a mature entrant to teaching after having her family. I remember her struggling courageously through her years of training. Now she has lost the hour-every-fortnight of non-contact time that she used to get, and although she still loves the teaching and the children, she hates all the paperwork and she cannot bear to think about next year's OFSTED inspection . . .

On top of everything else, yesterday a parent upset her by ringing her to complain because she had told his child not to suck her thumb while she was talking to her – he said it would cause her to be bullied.

'It's quite dreadful', she says, 'we are not even supposed to comfort a child these days. Do you know even female teachers are advised not to help a child who has messed herself without someone else being present?'

I agree it is quite dreadful. Yes, I'm fuming again. It is the familiar story, six years after getting her long-dreamt-of qualification, she now dreams of getting out of teaching as soon as she can.

I tell her how we GPs are advised by academics and by our protection societies never to examine a woman without a chaperone present. But what would be the result of that, I say, if you actually started to do it? It would soon be thought unusual or even suspicious if you didn't, and inevitably sometimes there wouldn't be a chaperone available. Soon you wouldn't be able to be alone with a woman at all, or a child, and soon after that you wouldn't be able to be alone with a man either. Then you would need a second chaperone to guard against the accusation that you and the first chaperone were in cahoots. Perhaps the answer would be to invite the whole waiting-room in to join the party. Anybody out there think I'm joking?

We are in complete agreement that in the end you have to trust people, and she leaves with her examination (unchaperoned), her prescription for six months of HRT, and her weary laugh.

The end of the morning . . .

That is the end of surgery, but the daily post brings more. The first madness is the sheer bulk of the correspondence. Letters getting longer and longer and arriving later and later. They are so massive and comprehensive (the record-holder ran to eight A4 sheets, all of which we are obliged to file and keep for the rest of the patient's life) that they take weeks to get dictated and typed. Meanwhile the patients are being discharged from hospital earlier and earlier, often with no information at all, often still in the throes of the illnesses for which they were hospitalised, and we are left having to try to get through on the telephone to obtain basic information that is essential for their continuing care. This situation seems to have got worse since the widespread introduction of specialist communication officers on the wards. Consultants' secretaries, always the communications linchpin in the past, are now for much of the time replaced by answerphones, and the tapes on the answerphones are increasingly often full – so the efficiency drive goes on.

After the clinical correspondence there is another bundle of glossy brochures about the latest additions to the ranks of mysteriously entitled bodies jostling with one another to regulate us – the National Institute for Clinical Excellence (NICE), the Commission for Health Improvement (CHI), primary care groups, Caldicott Guardians and clinical governors.

Now Jenny, the practice nurse who does the leg ulcer clinic, wants to talk to me about the impossibility of implementing the 68 pages of guidelines for leg ulcer management which have just been issued by a committee of the local health authority. She says that doing the preliminary assessment properly would take 45 minutes for every patient, and she has a great many other things to do which seem to her to be more important. I say that I will write for clarification. (I did, but I never received a reply – everyone too busy, probably.)

Over coffee the talk is of an ambulance service that seems more concerned with collecting statistics than patients, and of hospitals that are so short of beds that it is extremely difficult to get patients in, but which have so many regulations surrounding the discharge process that once they are there it is extremely difficult to get them out again. This is even when we, the people who are going to be looking after them and who have often known them for years, insist that it will be perfectly safe to do so.

Finally, I tell the story we heard last night from our friends, Judith and Edward, who had just been visiting their daughter in a maternity hospital in London. They had had to wait for some time at the door of the hospital in the driving April sleet for their ringing of the security bell to be answered. By the time they had been identified as legitimate visitors to their new grandson, Ben, a substantial queue of muffled, shivering and stamping people had formed in the snow behind them. Then when the door latch eventually clicked open, the whole queue just followed them in. While they stood meekly at the reception desk waiting for the next stage of their security clearance, everyone else just walked past them and dispersed into the building.

'*But*', said Judith triumphantly (because she knows I appreciate this sort of thing), 'everything is all right, the hospital has a security system *in place*'.

Nothing can possibly go wrong . . .

Something peculiar is going on

You may think it is an exaggeration to juxtapose these examples in a single morning, but actually it is the other way round: I couldn't possibly tell you the half of it, there are far more of them going on all the time than I could describe here.

My wife and I bought a table-lamp in a sale at a shop in Guildford. It was the last they had of a particular model, and we said we would be happy to take the lamp on display, which was plugged in and shining brightly. The first thing the salesman did when packing it up was to start to remove the plug, so I asked him to leave it on, please, because we would need it, too. He replied that he had to take it off because he had fitted it himself and he did not have the necessary qualification. Even though his skill in this rather elementary area of modern life (he was, after all, a salesman in an electrical department) had obviously been good enough for his shop, its customers and its insurers. Even though I said that I would be prepared to take responsibility in writing, and actually produced a sheet of paper and a pen in order to do so. Even though the plug had been operating safely for however long the lamp had been on display. Even though I was going to put it straight back on when we got home, and I wasn't qualified either. No, he was sorry, it was the rule, and off came the plug.

One of the most intelligent, experienced, respected and beloved community nurses in our area telephoned me while I was writing this chapter, heard what I was writing about and agreed, 'Yes, I am finding this very, very difficult at the moment. I have just been told I'm "living in the dark ages". That doesn't do much for your confidence.'

Something peculiar is going on because I do believe, as I have said earlier, that each of these situations, which from our perspective down on the ground floor of life seems utter madness, appears to be essential, inevitable good sense to reasonable people acting in good faith who see things from an entirely different perspective.

The point about the madness is that each problem is insignificant *on its own*. It is only people who have to put it all together into a whole that actually works who can see the problem – each irritation, looked at by itself, seems self-evidently and *indisputably* to be progress. It seems ludicrous and irresponsible to question any specific example. It is only from the generalist perspective, which confronts life as an integrated whole, that the madness becomes visible *at all*.

The purpose of this book is to try to explain the difference between these two views of life, and to find the origins of this state of affairs in which the real people who actually do the things that matter in life have become so humbled, demoralised and devalued by the inhumanity of system.

A world that expects a teacher to put the implementation of a *rule* that says they must not comfort a child above, of all things, *comforting a child*, is a world that has gone completely mad.

> What you call madness is not mad to me
> Perceptions vary with your point of view
> All things look different when you climb the tree
> The captain's view is different from the crew.
> I'm sure you really understand my aim
> With lives at stake you can't leave things to chance.
> If standards slip it's me who'll get the blame
> So let me play my tune and you just dance.
> OK, drug-safety warnings drive you mad
> And you think crying 'wolf' is doing harm.
> You say that doing too much good makes bad
> And only fools keep raising false alarm.
>   But one thing I am sure we can agree;
>   If you were here, you'd be as mad as me.

CHAPTER THREE

The nature of authority has changed

There's a girl in my class who's got an uncle aged two. She tells him off instead of **him** *telling* **her** *off.*

'Do you smoke?'
  'Of course not, I stopped when you told me to, 12 years ago.'

You're always so nice I don't take any notice of you.

All changed, changed utterly?

'You are writing a book.'
  'You are a doctor...'
Everybody seems to take it for granted that both writing a book and being a doctor require authority. Indeed, they often assume that doing either of these things is *of itself* a sign of having authority, and is therefore both desirable and admirable.

However, the world is changing. In fact, the world *has* changed. As someone who is trying to do both of these things at the moment, I find that authority, which I do indeed require if I am to stand any chance of being successful in either role, is being fundamentally undermined. The new culture which is sweeping the world seems to have left people like me, who take the broad, unfocused, non-classically academic approach, in writing just as much as in medicine, without a leg to stand on.

Yet the kind of medicine I and many colleagues try to practise as this kind of doctor, and the kind of issues I am trying to address as this kind of writer, simply cannot be tackled in a narrow, focused, classically academic way. However, and I say this with all humility, they do need to be tackled with authority. So how am I going to find a way out of this conundrum?

Let me start by looking at the radical change that has taken place in society's attitude to authority.

What on earth has changed?

'We can no longer duck legislation on euthanasia.' So said a leader in the *Independent* newspaper on the day after the Newcastle GP, Dr David Moore, had been acquitted of murder after having given a dying patient a large dose of diamorphine.[11] The case had been brought solely because the doctor, bravely or foolishly according to your point of view, had told the press exactly what he had done.

> *We can regret the passing of the world of complicity. The world in which we now live will not allow it. . . . The law will have to be clarified and the Government will have to bring in new legislation.*[12]

This is one example, selected simply because it is current as I write, of what are almost daily examples of an assumption that something absolute has changed, and changed recently, in our society: 'The world in which we now live will not allow it.'

Why not, when – and the implication is quite clear – it has always allowed it before? What has changed? Why has it changed just now? What is so special about this particular tick of the mighty clock of history? Perhaps most interestingly of all, why is this extraordinarily profound change so little discussed and so little questioned when the questioning and evaluation of new ideas are exactly what the change itself is supposed to be about? What is there about this particular innovation which evokes such blind faith in its rightness, such unquestioning belief that it is inevitable, such an assumption that it is progress?

Ready about . . . Why?

The quote at the head of this chapter about the little girl who could 'tell off' her baby uncle illustrates what an early grasp we have of authority (not to mention what an early grasp we have of paradox).

We learn the rules young, based on factors such as age, family position and body mass, and on the whole we obey them, or at least we know that we are *supposed* to obey them. As time goes on, our conception of authority becomes more complicated and we begin to enter a stage of healthy questioning. We begin to ask why we should pay attention to what other people say, and still more why we should act upon it.

You might think that being the captain of a boat is the supreme example of someone with clearly defined authority ('Walk the plank.' 'Yes, sir, of course sir,' and that sort of thing). But that wasn't the way it worked when I was on a sailing holiday with a crew of teenage daughters. Here it was not so much the 'Ready about ... Lee-o,' used by generations of skippers to perform an exquisitely co-ordinated tack. Instead we used the more democratic 'Ready about ...', 'Why, Dad?' model, which was followed by a chaotic scene involving shouting, whizzing ropes and close encounters with alien craft more often than by the smooth change of course I had anxiously planned.

The girls were just growing up, of course. And perhaps democratic society is just growing up. Perhaps it has now reached a healthily questioning stage of *its* development, and everyone is quite properly having to explain 'why' before the hard-faced jury of depersonalised corporate wisdom.

If that is the case, then we are in a terrible muddle.

Parents' authority undermined

The relationship between the parent and the child is the beginning of all authority, and we are in a terrible muddle about parental authority. The consequences as I see them affecting my patients are anything but funny. I see parents increasingly subjected to draconian authority from the state, while their authority over their own children has been substantially taken away. At the same time, society continues to hold them responsible for their children's behaviour.

I am not talking here about rare events highlighted by the selective attention of the media; I am talking about my personal experience. I have seen parents arrested on four separate occasions on the same day that their children (in one case an adopted child) made allegations of minor physical correction. Each time it took many months to get their parental rights restored. These were not abusing parents, whom I abhor as vehemently as anybody does. They were people much like you and me – friends of mine.

Teachers' authority undermined

I see the same strange contradictions applying to the authority of schoolteachers. One retired teacher I know was recently persuaded to return for half a day to fill in for a sudden sickness absence. At one point in the lesson he found himself taking, he momentarily touched the shoulder of a girl who was being outrageously rude. He describes the chattering class immediately freezing to galvanised attention and saying, as with one voice, 'You can't do that, sir, you can't *touch* us'. The kids know exactly who has the whip hand now.

These children, who are tested by the state as no children have ever been tested before, seem to have almost no experience of authority at a personal level. Yet their teachers, who are the butt of perpetual denigration in the media, are themselves subject to machine-like authority whenever suspicions are raised against them. At the same time, these teachers are somehow expected to exert control, armed with nothing but what managers airily describe as charisma, whilst those same managers openly thank God they have left front-line teaching themselves.

Patients' authority undermined

I see the same strange contradictions applying to the authority which patients are allowed to exercise over their own lives. Something has changed here as well. Compliant, law-abiding citizens have recently been forced by legislation into buying their aspirins a few at a time in tiny, expensive packs. My mother used to buy them by the thousand. One of my patients saw immediately how easy it would be for anyone to buy a lethal dose, despite the new regulations, merely by visiting several chemists in succession. 'You wonder who runs the country, don't you', he said, 'I could do it better myself'.

Meanwhile, I try to persuade people with coronary artery disease that it is important for them to take an aspirin every day for the rest of their lives. And all of this against a background of global lawlessness such that television documentaries tell us that the world as a whole spends more money on illicit drugs than on food.

Who can blame authority, one might almost think, if it feels the need to prove its potency by keeping its few remaining compliant citizens jumping though ridiculous hoops? It is pathetically easy to regulate the conscientious, law-abiding workers who are honestly trying to do a good, relatively unselfish job.

One thing is certain, something peculiar is going on, and it isn't just something that *they* are doing to *us*, it is also something that we are *all* to a greater or lesser extent doing to *ourselves*. It is extremely difficult to pin down what it is, but it has something to do with our communal loss of confidence in the authority of common sense.

Another contradiction?

Here is another highly significant contradiction. The change we are considering is all about life feeling as if it is becoming more and more controlled, yet in the past many aspects of life were unquestionably *more* controlled and more authoritarian than they are today, not less so. An old lady died in Alton quite recently who had been put into the workhouse as a teenager by her mother because she was 'in moral danger'. (The Alton Workhouse, once notorious for its harsh regime, and still one of the finest buildings in the town, has now been converted into comfortable accommodation for elderly people.)

Perhaps all that has really changed is that we now have greater *expectations* of freedom, and it is in comparison with those expectations that we feel let down. Because increased personal freedom was at the centre of what we imagined progress to be *about*. Wasn't it?

Or perhaps the change is something else again. Could it simply be that technology has allowed us to apply rules much more thoroughly than was possible in the past, so that even though the old rules appear harsh to us, in reality there was always a great deal of slackness in their application? Most of the time perhaps, and for most of the people, the saying that 'rules are made to be broken' really did mean just that. Another old lady surprised me, years ago, by telling me that in her youth (now a century or so ago) there were parts of Alton where policemen always walked in pairs, otherwise the rowdies knocked their helmets off – not quite the image we normally have of an authoritarian past.

Ideas-led or tools-led change?

Freeman Dyson in his book *Imagined Worlds*[13] lists the great innovations of history and shows that although we assume they are driven by new ideas, in fact it is four times more common for them to be driven by new *technology*. So perhaps the fundamental change we are now seeing is that for the first time tools have arrived which enable us *really* to put rules into practice, without exception and without fail. Perhaps this change has come about not because it is a good idea (as we like to think), but much more prosaically because it is now, for the first time, technically *possible*.

Just as architecture moves to exploit the potential of every advance in structural technology, giving us Gothic cathedrals in one age and extravagantly crafted, gravity-defying, silver-sheathed art galleries in another, so perhaps the structure of our society has now taken a quantum leap to a previously inconceivable level of analysis and control by authority, simply because information technology has become available to make it *possible* to make that leap. It has also led us collectively to the assumption that that individual human authority has been superseded, and to the assumption that we have moved – and none too soon – from a fuzzy old world of *subjective* authority to a bright, shining, dare I say 'brave' new world of *objective* authority.

Objective authority rules (OK?)

The idea that society's concept of authority has been profoundly influenced by the computer revolution fits well with the kind of change we have noted in the nature of authority. It is the absolute, fixed, measurable, provable, *objective* kinds of authority which have come to the fore, and the relative, unmeasurable, flexible, *subjective* kinds which have been routed.

The days when personal experience, judgement and integrity were paramount are gone. Now authority derives from a chain of formal verification. Once this idea gained a foothold, and once we had the technology (namely computers) to apply it, it swept all before it.

Some categories of authority

Subjective
- Trust authority
- Experience authority
- Tradition authority
- Moral authority
- Religious authority (faith)

Objective
- Legal authority (law)
- Position authority (status, age, rank)
- Management authority (line-manager, etc.)
- Contract authority (he who pays the piper . . .)
- Logic authority (formal reasoning, mathematics)
- Scholarship authority (reference to secure, acknowledged sources)

It did so because this type of authority has one incomparable advantage – it is *certain*. Any attempt to compare the certain with the uncertain is unbalanced; there is simply no contest. This explains why the revolution has come about so quickly, and why there has been so little intellectual opposition. There seems to be no intellectual argument that can be made. Like armoured Romans attacking naked tribesmen, there is no defence.

Objective authority derives from hard evidence that is verifiable in the outside world. The whole point about it is that it should be infallible. In other words, it should be *certain*. And if it is certain, it must be *unchallengeable*.

Subjective authority, on the other hand, derives from internal experience, wisdom, judgement and integrity. It is unmeasurable, unprovable and fallible. It is therefore *uncertain* and *challengeable.* This, simply and starkly, is the measure of the difficulty which we share when we try to justify our feelings, however intense and desperate those feelings may be, that the changes we are experiencing are having hidden side-effects which, in critical areas to do with life itself, are outweighing the all too obvious good that they do.

'Trust me, I'm a doctor'

GPs are responsible for the 'everything' in medicine, and for much outside it. They have to deal with the 'everything' in a way which inspires confidence and *deserves* to inspire confidence, the latter being more difficult but ultimately more important. 'Trust me, I'm a doctor' is well chosen as the title of a television series that raises healthy questions about the medical myth, but the saying reflects the general understanding that it is part of the *function* of a doctor to be trusted.

For most patients, having a doctor who inspires confidence is their top priority – higher even than having one who is 'nice'. Surveys which show that a high proportion of patients think doctors are trustworthy, as surveys invariably do, are the equivalent of surveys which show that a high proportion of motorists believe that their cars have wheels. It goes with the job ... 'Trust me, I'm a lawyer' would be a different kind of joke.

Yet people worry about how doctors (doctors in general, that is – they have a touching and significant tendency to make an exception of their *own* doctor) can keep abreast of advances in medicine in order to justify this trust, seeing that they are neither experts nor specialists of any kind. Surely everyone has to specialise these days? How can GPs possibly maintain a valid overview in something as vast as modern medicine? From whence, the question is asked ever more insistently in the modern world, do generalist doctors get their *authority?*

In truth, the situation is even worse than people think. The profound change that takes place in doctors as they mature from being trainees who learn theory and do things 'by the book', into independent professional practitioners who make judgements on the basis of a sophisticated and constantly evolving inner understanding, represents nothing less than a graduation from the one kind of authority to the other.

But we have a problem here, because the graduation is the wrong way round. The world, as we have said, is going – has gone – from subjective to objective, but here are doctors graduating from objective to subjective. And to complicate things still further, patients want the best of both worlds. They want a young doctor who is 'up to date', but they also want one who is mature, 'experienced' and 'wise'.

Evidence-based medicine

Riding over the horizon to solve this problem has come the United States Cavalry of Evidence-Based Medicine (EBM). The self-proclaimed revolution has been largely missed by patients, despite its being the Biggest By Far (BBF) of the Big New Ideas (BNIs) of medicine in the 1990s. This is because lay people tend to think that medicine was already based on evidence. Dr Martyn Evans, a healthcare philosopher, said as much at the 1997 Spring Symposium of the Royal College of GPs, in Swansea:

> *A layman like me finds this rather upsetting. For instance, I find myself wondering why basing clinical decisions on evidence is thought either new or exciting, and, by implication, anxiously pondering what it was that clinical decisions used to be based on before this big idea.*

But now I am suggesting an explanation – we are talking about a different *kind* of evidence. We are talking now about 'real' evidence – *certain* evidence. Clinical decisions were based on an authority before, sure enough, but it was a traditional kind of authority which is not so much being *challenged* as being *utterly discounted* in the official, received view of today.

Subjective authority (trust) still counts at the personal level

Back in surgery after that Spring Symposium two years ago (academic meetings for GPs are usually at weekends, so it is back to work the next day), we are back in the world of traditional authority.

Through a mixture of choice and necessity, EBM seems no more than a gleam in a distant, academic eye.

The patients, either because they are behind the times or because they know something the official world does not, by and large continue to trust us in the old-fashioned way. That doesn't mean that they don't occasionally bring bundles of printout from the Internet. Very occasionally, in fact. My experience is that this happens in about one of the 8000 or so contacts I have each year – far less often than they bring those warning sheets, and much less often than I suggest they look things up on the Internet. But even these patients still come for *something*, at least as much as other patients, and that something has a great deal to do with trust.

What is more, having seen both sides of the argument, I am convinced that they are right to be trusting. I trust my own doctor; I don't constantly question the basis on which he makes his opinions. I have confidence not only because I believe the confidence to be justified, but because I believe confident patients simply get better better. And that is what I want for me and my family. I do not want my doctor to treat me as a 'client', and not even on this occasion as a colleague – I want him to treat me as a patient. This arrangement has stood the test of time. It has its faults, which of course we must try to minimise, but at least we know what they are.

However, the medical Evidence movement takes a completely different view, and it takes it with the *certainty* which is characteristic of the new authority I am talking about. It insists that we should base everything we advise and everything we do on formal evidence that is independent of personal experience. That is the way in which medical students are now trained, and in which the professional bodies and the law now expect us to behave. Increasingly it is the only kind of medicine which can be defended in retrospect when things go wrong.

We really have arrived at a state of affairs in which it is not supposed to matter any more when a patient has died, provided that we have followed the rules.

Reading the *BMJ* 'properly'

The editor of the *BMJ* recently estimated that it would take 24 hours to read a single issue of his journal properly. My *BMJ* comes in the post every Friday, and it is clearly 'essential reading' for my project. For this year I am also getting the *Lancet* – the other British contribution to the world's 'big five' medical journals. It comes in the post every Friday as well, and it is just as relevant. An ear, nose and throat surgeon at a conference I attended (oh yes, I'm going to conferences as well) told us that he scans the contents list through the transparent mailing-cover, and if he doesn't see anything about throats, ears or noses, he throws the copy away unopened. But I can't do that, because I am a generalist and I am interested in everything.

There are a lot of other medical journals to read as well. I particularly enjoy my own columns in the *British Journal of General Practice* for a start, and there are numerous free journals paid for by drug advertising. Then I mustn't forget the daily newspaper, which seems to get bigger every day, and lay journals such as *New Scientist* and *Prospect*. And there are also books. I have a backlog I have been planning to read, and everyone I talk to seems to recommend another couple.

Then I have the catching up to do – a file of articles relevant to the project that I have collected over the years. After two days spent processing this collection, reading, scanning extracts into my computer, recording the reference information and finding everything fascinating (which was why I saved them in the first place), I realised that this job alone was going to take me far longer than the time I had available.

I found the process of collating the electronic notes that I had been making on my pocket computer over the years and collecting on my desktop machine more productive. I transferred them one by one, with increasingly well-practised movements of my mouse, into an ideas-organising program called *The Brain*. This program, which I obtained via the Internet for a modest fee from a website in California,[14] enables me to link ideas together into a kind of family tree – each 'thought' being linked to others as 'parents', 'siblings' and 'children'. I spent two and a half weeks working solidly at this job (it is the sort of mechanical job you really can stick at for 12 hours a day until your legs have forgotten they are attached to you), not only reviewing the ideas in my mind but creating a complex and flexible web which continues to evolve and which is my principal resource as I am writing now.

Perhaps the least instructive fact about this web of ideas is the one that is easiest to state – the number of individual 'thoughts' that it

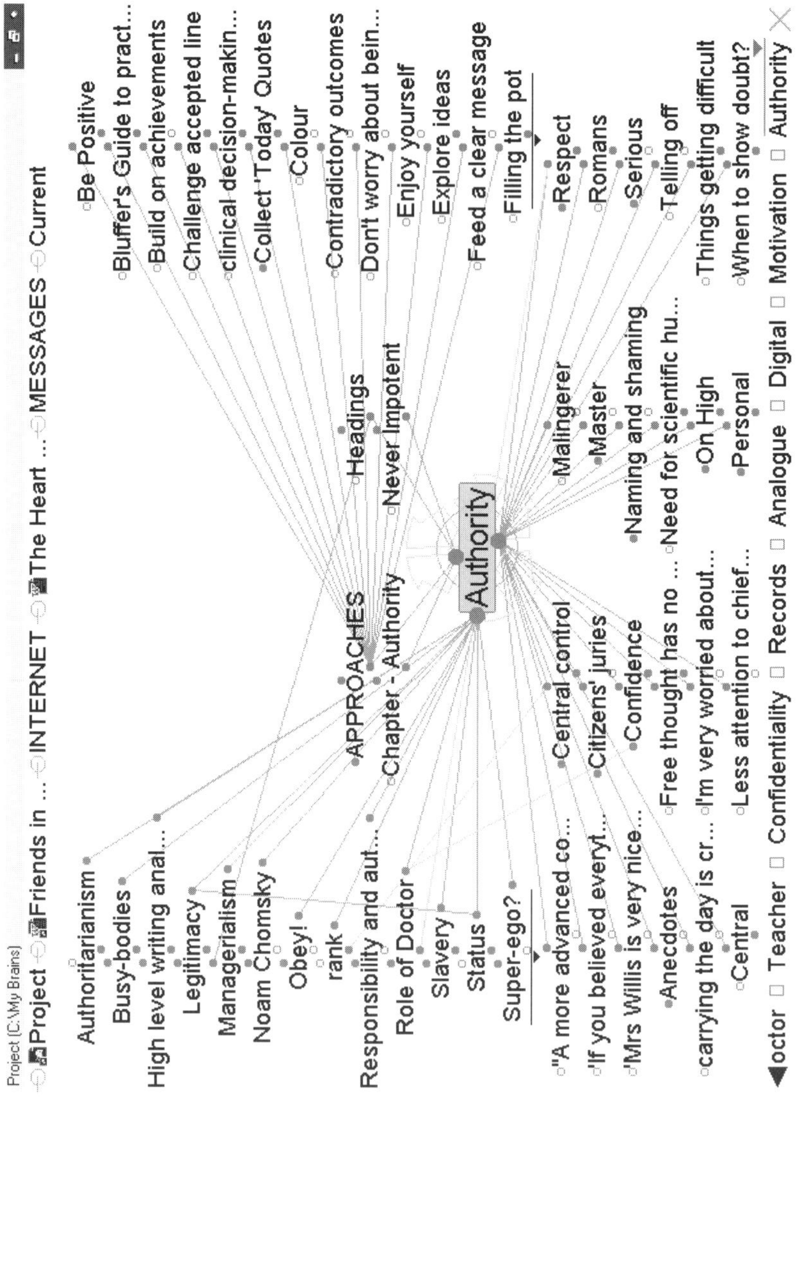

Figure 1 My 'brain' with *Authority* centre-stage.

contains. Each 'thought' can be a single word or a sentence, can have a piece of text (a 'note') attached to it, can be a link to a whole document (for example, one of them calls up the complete text of my previous book, and another my collection of patients' quotes), or a link to a website or even to another program. But *The Brain* continuously keeps track of how many of these 'thoughts' there are (I mean *exactly* how many). I've just looked, and the figure stands at 3288.[15]

The interesting thing to me is how many more this is than I would ever have guessed by looking at the relatively few that will fit on the screen, even though I entered every single one of them myself. It is a daunting insight into the magnitude of what I am trying to do – to assemble them all, or at least the sense of them all, into a single stream of words.

The problem of references

Having suggested the size of the problem of the background reading for a general project, I must come now to the problem of references. We all know that an authoritative book must be referenced. That is why I have just spent more than half an hour on the *BMJ*'s website trying to locate the reference to the editorial I just referred to, in which the editor estimated the time taken to read one issue properly (trying to do the thing properly, you see . . .).

In the event I haven't been able to find it, probably because the editorial, contrary to my recollection, dates from prior to January 1996 – the starting point of the electronic *BMJ*'s indexed, online archive.

So what shall I do now? Shall I ask the medical library to find it for me in an old-style, manual index? Does it matter? Would that be a good use of their time? Or of mine?

I doubt it. What would I do with it when I found it? Would anybody look it up, or would the little number in the text just stick its foot out and trip the reader up? Does it really matter anyway? Would it alter the point I am trying to make if it had actually been *12* hours that Richard Smith estimated it took to read the *BMJ*? Is his estimate actually any better than mine, which happens to be about the same? Both are only estimates, after all, and people will read at vastly different rates. So why mention his editorial at all? That's easy – it was his idea, not mine.

And even if I do quote a reference there is another danger – that people will simply be diverted into challenging the reference instead of thinking about the argument it was intended to support. So it goes on, another circle, round and round . . .

Therefore it seems to me that it is impossible to retain this kind of scholastic authority at the same time as taking the broad-brush approach. If you delve deeply into every aspect, you simply cannot cover the whole. Of course I could pursue the reference to that editorial, but if I attempted everything at that level of detail I wouldn't get past the foothills of the mountain I am trying to scale. I would be picking up the first pebbles I come to and putting them under a magnifying glass. I would be interested in that, too, but it isn't what I am trying to do. Once you try to deal with the whole of life instead of a restricted field, tracing everything to its source simply becomes impossible. However, if readers insist on a rigorous, evidence-based approach to everything that they are prepared to take seriously, then it seems to me that they will systematically exclude all attempts to deal with the whole of life.

Perhaps we can glimpse here one part of an explanation for the kinds of official madness we are examining.

A passionate belief in classical science

I am steering here a difficult middle course between equally dangerous misconceptions. Let me repeat with the greatest possible emphasis that I believe passionately in the importance of science and logic. The use of the word 'passion' in this context is deliberate. Even in the awesome, dispassionate presence of the words 'science' and 'logic', my experience as a GP gives me the courage to claim validity for *feelings* – and I mean feelings as a reliable reference, not as a vague 'flower-power'. I endorse the view of the 1960s Muscatine report to the University of Berkeley's Academic Senate quoted by Gunther S Stent,[16] which looks down a long, fastidious nose at the 'Beat' phenomenon that was sweeping that university at the time:

> *Students who hold the belief that feeling is a surer guide to truth than is reason cannot readily appreciate the University's commitment to rational investigation.*

The relevance of Penrose and Gödel

On the other hand, the more subtle point about the limits of formal logic that I am trying to make may, it seems to me, be consistent with the discussion of Gödel's theorem that I heard in a Gresham College lecture given by Professor Roger Penrose near the beginning of my sabbatical.[17] It was the same argument that he put as follows in his book, *The Emperor's New Mind*, and please stick with this bit, because it is crucial to my argument:

> *What Gödel showed was that any such precise ('formal') mathematical system of axioms and rules of procedure* **whatever**, *provided that it is broad enough to contain descriptions of simple arithmetical propositions (such as 'Fermat's last theorem'), and provided that it is free from contradiction, must contain some statements which are neither provable nor disprovable within the means allowed by the system.*

Penrose explains that although 'this is just a mathematical idealisation', its implication extends to the whole world and means that *any* formal (logical) system of thinking contains within it truths (true ideas) which will remain inaccessible to its own methods of analysis forever, however technically impeccable those methods of analysis may be.

In other words it is possible, to put it no more strongly, that the point of view which I am attempting to put forward has been excluded from the mainstream, despite every single one of us acknowledging its validity at some level of our experience, for a completely intractable yet none the less invalid reason. This is because it is a member of a class of truths which are inherently and permanently inaccessible to formal proof.

A doctor stood up at the back of a meeting when I had been talking about these things, and he said that it was a delight to hear Gödel's name being mentioned. Years previously he had started a degree in mathematics and spent the first term or so proving Gödel's theorem. He said (as other mathematicians I have spoken to agree) that the theorem proved rigorous (i.e. certain). Having realised the significance of this, he gave up mathematics for good and started medicine.

But I am glad that Roger Penrose did not give up mathematics when he encountered Gödel's theorem. The title of his lecture was 'The limits of computation', and he supported his message, under the elegant hammer-beamed roof of Staples Inn, with me in the fourth row, with many quite independent mathematical arguments. His conclusion, controversial although it undoubtedly remains, is of central importance in a world which increasingly believes that reality can be reduced to a mathematical equation. He says that it cannot, and that it's as simple as that. And I, for completely non-mathematical and permanently unprovable reasons, agree with him.

Something beyond

Joy Railton helped us at home one morning a week for more than 20 years, almost all of which were past normal retirement age. I remember coming back on one occasion while she was working, and apologising for leaving footprints across her newly washed quarry-tiles. 'I don't mind', she replied, not the least concerned. '*I* know I have done them'.

I was struck at the time by her assumption that she was answerable to an authority not just higher than us (her employers), but quite *different* to us. She had gone into service, like so many of her generation in this part of the world, on the evening of the day she left school at the age of 14, and she had been working continuously ever since. We used to think that the reason she went on coming to us after the children had gone was because she loved our dog, but she went on long after he died, and indeed long after she could manage our stairs. We thought it would be silly to install a stair-lift for her, so we took to cleaning upstairs ourselves (I say 'we' . . .).

But I would like to think I have just a little of Joy Railton's integrity. I would like to think that the NHS Executive will eventually decide that I have used my time on this study leave well. But the real judgement will be my own, made on the basis of principles, not political whims, fashionable ideas, protocols or formulae – answerable (and Joy would never have dreamt of saying this, but it is true) to something *beyond*.

The authority for what I say in this book is my personal experience of real life, reported as honestly as I can manage – not so much what I *hear* as what I *see*. That kind of authority has its own timeless validity, and it comes from a quarter of a century of experience as a family doctor, with all that that means in terms of intimate access to countless crucial episodes in the lives of people I know rather well (all set within the context, let us not forget, of a professional, scientific discipline). As a GP in the NHS I am one of the last autonomous professional generalists in the modern world, whose role bridges the art/science divide in a way that is now unique.

That is fair enough, but it leaves open the question of why I should report that experience, and why anyone should pay attention when I do so. And here again the answer is simple: every single one of us has the right and indeed the duty to report experience which conflicts with received wisdom and which we honestly believe warns of danger ahead. If something is wrong, it does not matter in logic who points it out. This is the essential appeal of the story of the Emperor's new clothes – the shattering of the mirror in which officialdom looks for dutiful collusion with even its most ludicrous ideas.

The Cambridge philosopher Geoffrey Lloyd has said that the ancient Greeks devised the logic and evidence-based arguments that we use today, not to create mathematics *per se*, but to give ordinary citizens the means and the confidence to participate in democracy.[18] They recognised that the empirical truth of a statement is independent of who it is that utters it.

To its credit, our society today prides itself on being unafraid of truth. If we are prepared to honour that high-sounding creed, then not even the least of us is entirely without authority.

Come, trust me, while I doctor, first your cat
and, second, the statistics that will show
the credulous insurance salesman that
some costly oil will make his coiffure grow.
And trust me, I'm a doctor, while I 'spin'
a subtle web to undermine the foe
who last week to my master's lynch was pin
but who, this week, my master will not know.
And trust me, I'm a Strangelove, I'm a Who,
I'm bargain-blighted Faustus, doomed to Hell.
I'm Doctor Crippen, cooking up my brew,
but not, in truth, to make you very well.
 The Doctor Jekyll record's strong B-side
 reveals the lurking face of Mister Hyde.

CHAPTER FOUR

Making models: structure and reality

'Mummy, why is she dressed up like a nurse?'
'She is a nurse, sweetheart.'

A famous modeller's feet of clay

Words are such clumsy things. The ones I am writing now are already crowding out the beautiful things that were filling my mind a moment ago. I can feel it happening, but I can't stop it. All I can do is keep going and try to express some of it, because what I want to say is important. And the difficulty of saying it is part of what I want to say.

People must have thought that yesterday's debate was important too – 'Is Science killing the Soul?' – The *Guardian*/Dillons Debate – Steven Pinker *v* Richard Dawkins. Westminster Central Hall was completely full. 2400 of us, so the chairman, Tim Radford, the *Guardian's* science editor, told us in his introduction . . .

The man on my right looks up from a little edition of something by Dawkins when I say something about the floor being full and how people are starting to pour up the staircases and out on to the balconies. Surprised, obviously, by my surprise. 'Dawkins is a draw'.

I nod. I knew that, but don't care to say it. His book seems more interesting than me – more intelligent.

All around *Guardian*s flutter – characterful, intelligent faces, interesting sweaters, fleeces in a 'natural' shade I haven't seen before – funny that, 'natural' fleeces (no one to share the joke).

A few woolly hats. Why have they all come? Which side are they on? I listen for the words of the animated conversation on my left for a clue. It is between two young men, one of them Chinese, with a perfect Oxford accent. He says that the organ pipes are the biggest he's ever seen. I can't resist joining in. Have they seen the Albert Hall? 'The pipes there make these ones look small.' 'Oh,' they smile, politely impressed – and go back to talking together. What is it he is saying? 'That's what is so wonderful about my particular relationship with God . . .' Right – no mystery there – 'Is Science Killing the Soul?' – two on the side of the soul . . .

To start with it isn't a debate. Dawkins admits this straight away. 'If two people are arguing passionately two completely different points of view, it does not always follow that the truth lies mid-way between them . . .' Brilliant white shirt, incredibly relaxed in front of the huge audience, not the slightest sign of nerves, completely confident that he knows his words (God, how does he do it?). 'And if two people are saying the same thing (he knows that we know that he means *him and Pinker*), it is possible they are both *right.*' He looks up and waits for the applause.

'Or both wrong,' I say aloud. No response from the neighbours on either side, and certainly no applause. OK, I won't do it again.

I close my Psion electronic organiser with its satisfying 'snap' and push it back inside the zip-folder on top of my warm, outdoor coat which is folded on my lap. Switched to its smallest font-size, with the screen tipped slightly away from me under the seat-back against my knees, I have been writing naughty, private things, funny sweaters and the conversation at my left shoulder being more noteworthy so far than what is being said on the stage. I've heard all that before, been spellbound by its clarity and force before, but now I've come to find out what it *means*. Dawkins doesn't seem to have any idea about that, despite being so sure.

Pinker on the other hand, says things I haven't heard. He can explain everything about the mind, everything about the way it works, as the function of a marvellous machine. A machine whose intricate workings he and Dawkins and I, for heaven's sake, and the chairman, and everybody else in the hall, unless they haven't been paying attention for the last few years, find utterly wonderful, beautiful, fascinating and awe-inspiring.

He also thinks that he can explain everything about the way we *feel*, but I'm not so sure about that. And he thinks, in answer to the chairman's question, that we can rationalise the remarkably uniform human idea of something which is good, or something which is 'God' if anyone prefers, as a construct only a little way beyond our imputing (a typically accurately chosen word) a consciousness similar to our own within anyone else we meet.

Come to think of it, it's a bit like me imputing a consciousness to whoever it is I am addressing these words to now. So it's a case of 'Hi there,' I suppose . . .

Anyway, the questioners from the floor don't stand a chance. What can they say, even when they've survived the laughter at their tiny, distant voices, ridiculous after the amplified tones of the speakers, redoubled when the microphone arrives to catch their dying words? A man on the balcony manages to make an interesting point about the brain being like a television set – which would convey a powerful illusion to anyone arriving from a different planet (and possessing the technology to arrive from a different planet, but not for some reason being able to understand television sets) that it is generating its sounds and pictures from within. But we know the truth about television sets, don't we? So perhaps we don't know the truth about something which is really *out there*, beyond our physical selves?

I want to hear what Dawkins thinks about this, but instead he tells a joke that he once heard about television sets, and signals for the next question. Obviously he doesn't think the question needs answering – different planets indeed.

No wonder there wasn't a debate. This reminds me of an old idea, born of some frustration of a similar kind, about a battle between Panzer Tanks and butterflies. Something, perhaps, about a couple of experts on 'how?' speaking to an appreciative audience who have mainly come because they are interested in 'how?', but with nothing at all to say to the ones who came because they want to know 'why?', except to confirm that the experts have nothing to say about 'why?', despite their brilliance. Which is where, and why, I came in.

We shuffle down the exit stairs and I am disappointed. I had expected to feel at home among fellow-readers of my regular newspaper, with a shared interest in the fascination of science. Instead I feel strangely disturbed and alienated. I catch the eye of the lady next to me. 'Why did so many people come?'. She smiles and moves away slightly. The old charm must be failing. I can't help thinking that a religious meeting (what was it Dawkins said? religions are just 'old cults'?), however loopy and irrational, would have been much friendlier than the frightening aridity of this lot, but I don't suppose it matters. I walk away from the entrance looking straight ahead.

I pick my way through slower walkers as we go round Parliament Square, through the scaffolding and over the temporary pavement where most of the throng are pouring into Westminster tube station, which is being rebuilt underneath Big Ben. Huge, freshly gilded face, floodlit high above, with hands showing plenty of time to walk to Waterloo station. Backbone shivering against the black night sky, I run for the green man signal and out into the fresh, crisp openness of Westminster Bridge, looking back at the Houses of Parliament and then over to the left, down the river to the City and St Paul's, 'All bright and glittering in the smokeless air.'[19] Backbone-shivering indeed.

An hour home on the train from Waterloo. Nearly trapped by the man opposite who wants to talk about the draught through the closed carriage window. The carriages are far too old (I agree). It would help to have more hair (I laugh). The shareholders are only interested in money (I scowl). The weather – enough, I drop my head into the magazine on my lap like a guillotined aristocrat. Now I'm doing it, keeping slightly distant. I dive into my review of laptop computers.

'Notebooks – the perfect twelve. Budget-beaters, desktop replacements and the sexiest ultra-slims'. I read the seductive detail until my balding companion gets out at Woking. 'Goodbye', we smile, and it's better than London already.

I model, therefore I am

The squirrel was back in our walnut tree this morning as we had breakfast. It always comes at this time of year. Too early for the nuts, but it was collecting something, that's for sure. I don't know whether it thinks much, or whether it thinks at all, but you don't have to be an expert to work out that it has a model of our garden in its mind, and that it has a model of the tree, so that it knows where to jump in that amazing way. It has a model of where its paws are in space, where its tail is and where the branches are, and it gets the whole thing together in a way which would be simply unbelievable if you didn't see it happening. Everything is moving – the paws, the branches, the tail, the wind – and the whole lot has to coincide when he lands, and all to form part of a smooth flow of co-ordinated action which includes the branches all the way to his goal – whatever the goal is, because it can't be the walnuts, as they won't be ripe for months.

I can't do this as well as Richard Dawkins,[20] but I can wonder at the process just as much as he does when I try to model the whole thing in words and in my mind.

Models seem to be better than the real thing

The idea I am trying to model in this book is really rather circular. It is that a powerful illusion operates to make us think that models of ideas (this book, for example) are much more like the ideas they represent than they really are – that they actually seem to *be* the idea, and that they seem to be *better* than the idea. And that this is an unavoidable and unavoidably hidden limitation. This applies even more to the models that society holds in common than it does to the models in our own minds, and the resulting illusion is the cause of much apparent madness in the contemporary world.

Our minds operate in such a way that models grab ideas and take them over, giving them a shape and a solidity which is false – useful, for sure, but false. Obviously useful but less obviously false. Like a Disney World reconstruction of the Wild West – convincing enough at first, until there is a bout of rain and you find piles of plastic raincoats coming out of service tunnels all over the OK Corral.

The idea I want to model is that it isn't good enough just to improve the model, to take away the plastic raincoats and let people get really wet, and spray the ever-smiling staff with authentic cattle-puncher stench. Even if you do, in a fundamental way it will still remain a model. I once heard it said that 'In Schubert's rain you get wet'. OK, good for Schubert, his is a better model – he is a genius of course, but it still isn't reality.

Differences between models and reality

Here are some of the differences between models and reality, off the top of my head. Sometimes that is the best way to work – prime the pot and then let it flow, let the thoughts pour out, trust them to come in a sensible order – not the right order, because there isn't one right order, and if it seems that I have found the one right order, that is an illusion. One of the illusions. One of the mistakes. The model can have only one shape, however complex and beautiful it may be. In the mind there is an infinity of possible ideas, held in a kind of shimmering co-existence. Forget for a moment how this happens, and forget that it can't happen in the model, but just believe that it is possible, that it does happen in the mind. That something odd is going on. *Very* odd – which is reminiscent of something Richard Feynman said about quantum mechanics – something about how if you aren't amazed by it you don't understand it.[21]

We are getting closer when we use a computer. Closer than a book, certainly, or closer than a lecture or a conversation. Closer than all the things which are restricted to a single-file procession of words, one after another, each evoking its pictures in the listener's mind, but with the order chosen by the speaker or the writer. I keep shying away from this monster *Structure*, tying down my beautiful, ephemeral, butterfly idea. I want it to shimmer and live, but I have to lock it up in words and fix it on the page. I want to fix it so that I can look at it, see where I have got it wrong and improve it. This is the basis of science – making a better and better description of the world, then making it better still, then making it better again.

But so much of the essence of butterflies depends on them being *alive*.

Of all the tools we have to make the model better, the computer must be the greatest advance since language and writing. Ever since I got my first computer and typed in the code of a primitive BASIC word-processor, my writing has been freed like a bird from a cage from the agony of endlessly discarding sheets in order to rewrite the first sentence.

Although many orders of magnitude larger, more complicated and more expensive than my first word-processor, the programs I am using now do basically the same thing. They are magic slates for grown-ups. You write ideas down in any order, with or without mistakes – the provisional, the pompous, the crazy (de Bono recommends writing crazy things because they are particularly likely to produce interesting and new ideas[22]). Then you can go on forever matching the words more and more closely to the thought that you are trying to describe.

You can use headings and subheadings. The outliner function of the word-processor enables you to collapse the text out of sight for an overview, and you can change things around, fiddling with structure and word order indefinitely, looking for inconsistencies and resolving them, developing the idea – like having a conversation with the computer, like modelling in clay.

You can split a computer model anywhere, like that origami figure which opens and opens and opens. Once I was stuck when writing an article, and decided to clarify things by writing its last sentence first. Then I saw that the sentence I had written contained two ideas, so I split it. Then I made each new sentence into a paragraph, and before long the whole article had grown from that final sentence.

I was explaining this to a friend who said, 'So you can write it from the inside, can you?'

And I said, 'Yes, that's exactly what you can do.'

'The brain' again

The new class of ideas-modelling programs, of which *The Brain*, which I am using to organise some of my background material, is an example, take things further still. Much more like the real thing, much more like getting really wet in the plastic/smiling, smelly/tame, Wild West. If used to the full these programs can link up everything in your computer into an enormously complex network.

I found myself describing this web of ideas to a friend at the time when I had been absorbed in the process of creating it for two whole weeks. He guessed that one benefit from my effort would be that I would be able to print the whole thing out – in the same way that he could print a neat chart of the whole family tree he was constructing at the time using a genealogical program.

I hadn't thought of this, and I tried to picture how I would print out 3000 thoughts, each connected to anything up to 30 others, even without the text and/or complete documents which so many had attached to them. It was immediately obvious that to do this on a two-dimensional sheet of paper would be impossible, but I began to wonder if I could, in principle, do it in three dimensions.

A picture of an impenetrably tangled ball of threads came into my mind and made me realise that even if it would be possible to construct such a thing in physical reality, it would be useless. For a start, nothing but the small part of it which happened to be on the surface would be visible at all. And the centre, the part I would be most interested in, would be the most deeply hidden part of all. Not only that, but the whole thing would be fixed permanently in the one configuration, unless the connections could in some way be temporarily taken apart for it to be reoriented and then connected up again. Yet in its present electronic form I can display any one of an almost infinite variety of configurations at the merest whim.

The 'Wander' function on the 'Options' menu of *The Brain* does just this. Of little practical use, except to demonstrate the aptness of its name, but in a kind of joyful celebration of its own flexibility, *The Brain* will move randomly from one thought to another, about once every second, with the linked thoughts I have set up elegantly rearranging themselves on the screen as it does so.

Two pins in the idea

At this point I have reached two conclusions.

First, a physical model of an idea is not just a difficult thing to make, it is an *impossible* thing to make – a conceptual absurdity. There is a barrier to making such a thing which is as absolute as the barrier which prevents one from making an accurate map of the globe on a flat sheet of paper.

Secondly, electronic computers seem to be a much better bet as a way of modelling my big idea. They provide the ability to link everything together into a web which has no beginning and no end, and in which anything can come to the centre and become the focus of attention. Thus everything is changeable and everything is provisional, yet at the same time everything is fixed.

Clearly a physical model of my idea which I can make, pick up and hold is out of the question, so perhaps this 'virtual', electronic model is what I need. Or is that a conceptual absurdity as well?

My answer is that this more sophisticated model and the reality it represents look similar but are also fundamentally different. And the similarity is an even more powerful and therefore even more dangerous illusion. The danger arises principally because the same illusions which I can see when I play with models of my own thinking apply even more powerfully to the models which society makes of the ideas which it holds in common.

The rulers and administrators of society deal largely, and sometimes exclusively, with models, and they are sure that this is progress. They are inclined to think that their models are more real than the reality which they describe.

Deeply mysterious effects

They shut the road through the woods
Seventy years ago.
Weather and rain have undone it again,
And now you would never know
There was once a road through the woods.[23]

Rudyard Kipling's poem leads me into a further stage of the comparison between the ideas I am expressing and the models I am using to do so. For the idea in the mind sometimes seems like a wood or a forest, with innumerable paths going through it. The paths are numberless, as I discussed in *The Paradox of Progress*, because they are not discrete entities, they do not have clear boundaries, and they are all expressed in terms of one another. Numbering them would be meaningless, even though my computer model of a brain numbers its 'thoughts' so readily. But as we think of new ideas our brains seem to hold all the open possibilities in a kind of shimmering co-existence until we select one of them, when in an instant all of the others evaporate.

There is something which seems to be evocative of the quantum world in this. It certainly seems plausible that, as we are thinking, any number of feasible possibilities are being held, like the mutually incompatible fates of Schrödinger's imaginary cat,[24] in quantum superimposition, until the instant when we make a choice between them. This would account (as Roger Penrose once again pointed out) for the subjective impression that flashes of intuition really are instantaneous. It would also account for the observation that ideas lose so much of their richness as soon as we begin to write them down.

We look back and we see the one path we have followed through the wood, and all the possibilities that were open ahead as we moved forward have now disappeared and are irrelevant, as if they had never been. But we live life looking forward at endless, open possibilities all the time.

That is a reality we can never model.

> I'll make a concrete model of a cloud.
> I want a thing to hold, and feel, and save.
> My concrete models make me very proud,
> I know they'll bring me fame beyond the grave.
> It lends itself because it's cold and grey.
> You'd never guess how soft I make it look.
> The fact is, clouds are better done my way;
> I do the finest cloudscapes in the book.
> Real clouds evaporate but mine will last,
> Real clouds are priceless, mine are bought and sold,
> Real clouds make rain but mine make money fast,
> The silver lining of my cloud is gold.
>   And yet, although I wouldn't say it loud,
>   There's something *wrong* about a concrete cloud.

CHAPTER FIVE

Modern life is even fuller than we think it is

'My hearing's gone the other way, Dr Willis. I can hear things in the distance very acute.'
'That's an unusual complaint.'

Morning tea

'I don't think the chapter I was working on yesterday really worked – so I've stuck it in a separate file in the computer called "Useful bits chopped out".'

Lesley laughs as she passes me what's left of the tea.

'It was about how full life is, but I'm not sure that it's worth a chapter to itself, people know all about it already. I think I'll just cover the point as I go along . . .' She nods and indicates the bit she is reading from *Dogbert's Top Secret Management Guide*,[25] lent to me by a friend who has experienced the madness as a statistician in the recently modernised Forestry Commission:

> *Doctors are among the most motivated workers in the world. They work very long hours in return for incredible amounts of money and the opportunity to heal sick people. Obviously their motivation comes from their desire to work long hours.*

'That's incredible,' I say, 'look what I've just been writing in my notebook: "Doctors are one of the few groups who can be seen to be doing things other than medicine without worrying that people won't think they are busy enough".'

'Incredible. Do you write anything else in that notebook – anything about the family or anything . . . ?'

'No – not really – just thoughts about the project.'

She looks in resignation at the pile of books on my knees.

I pick up one from the bedding – *From Novice to Expert: Excellence and Power in Clinical Nursing Practice*[26] lent to me last week by a community nurse, another friend who has experienced the madness. 'Here she is saying that the nursing profession will only get the respect it deserves when it learns to define exactly what it is doing.' I read a passage I have marked:

> *A wealth of untapped knowledge is embedded in the practices and the 'know-how' of expert nurse clinicians, but this knowledge will not expand or fully develop unless nurses systematically record what they learn from their own experience.*

We nod at each other – the same old problem.

'But look here,' I say, turning to a second marker:

> *Hubert and Stuart Dreyfus[27] reported some air force studies that demonstrated that only by dropping the rules can one become really proficient. They cite the example of undergraduate pilots who are taught to follow a fixed sequence of visual scanning of instruments and dials. The air force researchers found that the instructors who were issuing these rules could find errors in the visual displays much more quickly than the trainees. They wondered whether the instructors applied the rules more quickly and more accurately than the student pilots, so they checked their eye movements and found that the instructors weren't using the rules that they were instructing the trainees in at all. Furthermore, their deviation from the rules allowed the instructors to perform faster and better.*

The same old conflict . . .

'Actually, I think there *is* something new that I can say about the fullness of life,' I say, as we get out of bed. 'It's this thing about the *double* failure of perception: not just that life is even busier and fuller than we think it is, but that *in spite of that* our minds cope far better than we think they do.'

Lesley knows what I mean and she agrees – which is reassuring, because when she doesn't she says so . . . keeps me on the rails.

'You know, I couldn't do this without you, talking things over with you like this; it's the most useful thing of all . . .'

Quite a bundle of things to carry downstairs, another book on the go at the moment, *Paradoxes of Progress* by Gunter Stent,[28] lent to me by an academic doctor in Newcastle who is another constant source of support and inspiration and more unflinching criticism.

Last week's *BMJ* and *Lancet* are high in the jumble of waiting correspondence on the table in the hall. Out of their wrappers but not much more yet, with three days to go before the next batch arrives.

I make space on the desk in the study. Piles of books on the floor, folders, things waiting to be scanned into the computer, sorted, put away, selectively culled. That's the big idea. Filing-cabinet drawers are open. The four new shelves I put on the wall so recently are already as full as the others, with books, magazines, reports, papers, packed in tightly.

Not quite 'paperless', my office, yet.

Not that it lacks computers. I have started using my desktop and my laptop machines alternately, so I can work in different places and positions. This means my legs still function in the evening. The laptop has a label on the keyboard which says 'IMPORTANT NOTICE; For comfortable and safe use, please read the Safety and Comfort Guide', which I don't think I've ever actually seen, but if it turns up I'll put it on the list of bedside reading perhaps. Meanwhile I have solved the fizzy-legs problem in my own way.

△ IMPORTANT NOTICE

For comfortable and safe use of this book please read the Safety and Comfort Guide.

COMING SOON: Guidance for comfortable and safe use of the Safety and Comfort Guide.

One advantage of using both machines is that every time I change I have to copy my current files – the working copy of this text in

Word, the database of notes transferred from my Psion pocket computer in Access, and my invaluable time-planner chart in Excel – so that I automatically have three recent copies of them all – one on each machine and the one on the floppy disk I use for the transfer.

My 'brain' program stays on the desktop machine because it is far too large to fit on a floppy. My old collection of 'thoughts, quotes and snippets', another 60 000 words (another countable thing), is in a Word file on both machines, where I also have accessible archives of almost everything I have ever written. Reference CDs, Internet access, and email are mainly on the desk machine, and so on – tools for driving pegs into my nebulous idea.

Out, now, for my ten-minute run on the hill (alternate mornings these days – after a long gap when I nearly stopped, I find this better than trying to run every day), and while I am out in the fresh air the whole plan for the chapter is clear in my head. I know just what to do – just describe what this morning is really like, how much is going on, all the threads. What could be simpler or clearer?

I run on, rehearsing the words carefully in my mind, and – about time, too – for my songs in the Operatic Society's Summer Show in (only) two weeks' time. That's after next week (Lesley's half-term) with the boat in Cornwall. 'I can give you the starlight, love unchanging and true . . .' Ivor Novello – wonderful song. As old as the hills of course. 'Hills? Pools? Blue?' That's it. The second line: 'I can give you the mountains, pools of shimmering blue . . .'

Gorgeous, sloppy stuff – you could only get away with it in an amateur show.

My notebook is still with me at breakfast in my running things. I flip through the morning paper: *Freedom of information, Escalating war in Kosovo, Rugby captain sacked for taking drugs*, with letters from people with different reasons why he shouldn't have been . . .

Things to remember today – we can't find the negatives of the canal holiday photographs Lesley wants to blow up for Judith's birthday. She has hunted through drawers, despite labelling (we could spend hours organising and labelling them better, we think, and still not have been able to find them), so can Colab make a decent enlargement from the print? I've said I'll ring and find out. We need someone to mow the lawn once while we are away next week, or we'll come back to a meadow. We mustn't forget to warn the cleaning lady when she comes this morning that we are going to be away.

Off to *Copenhagen*[29] this evening when Lesley finishes work. It is Michael Frayn's play about uncertainty and quantum physics and the mystery of human motivation, used by Iona Heath in her William Pickles lecture. She has been telling me for months that it is a *must* for this study-leave project.

So, having started the morning deciding I had nothing new to say about the fullness of life, I have spent the whole of it writing about it anyway.

The size of the problem

A few years ago it was fashionable to predict that by the end of the century (i.e. by *now*) we would all be suffering the embarrassment of too much leisure. It doesn't seem to have worked out like that. Today we seem to have two choices – we can be ill from overwork or we can be unemployed.

The experts seem to have been as bad at predicting the future as they usually are. All the greatest events – the microelectronics revolution, the collapse of the Communist Empire in Europe, the fragmentation of nation states (as opposed to their predicted amalgamation), the growth of fundamentalist religion, the retreat from rationality – took us completely by surprise.

So labour-saving devices have not saved labour by speeding up jobs, because we just pack our lives with new jobs, also speeded up, which we didn't do before. Word-processors have not made typists' lives easier, because they have just enabled employers to manage with fewer typists, and those that remain are busier than ever, being expected to perform all the functions of a publishing house, art studio and statistical service 'at the touch of a button'. The building of new motorways may have ended the annual nose-to-tail crawl to Cornwall, but now we crawl there three abreast any weekend we choose.

However, the problem I am talking about is not so much that our lives are full – we are choking, we can't breathe. The problem is that this is happening *disproportionately* to people doing front-line, general jobs, and that it doesn't *show* from the outside. That makes it all the more remarkable that so many people doing these jobs cope as well as they do, and that, provided they are allowed personal control of their work,[30] they thrive so much on the challenge.

At all magnifications the view is the same

'I say, Doctor – they say there's a terrible strain of flu out in China. A little boy of three died. Yes, three.'
  'In **China** *. . .?'*
. . . pause . . .
  '. . . Oh, I think they tell it you to frighten you.'

Evolution has equipped us, to an extent which seems hard to explain, with bodies and minds flexible enough to thrive in the grossly unnatural world we now inhabit. Of course, there is the 'anthropomorphic principle' which states that if nature had not so equipped us then we wouldn't be discussing the fact that it had. It is only survivors who tell their story. But the way that the physical and mental capacities that evolved in a natural environment have grafted smoothly on to technological enhancements such as motor-vehicles, telephones, telescopes and computers is truly astonishing.

However, it would be even more astonishing if evolution had provided this ability with no disparity at all. We are good at judging how far it is across a ravine we are thinking we might jump, and it is all too obvious how such an ability must have evolved. But no evolutionary pressure has ever operated to give us a similar ability to judge the scale of a threat we see through a telescope, a newspaper article, a television report or the Internet. And when we apply the mental processes which have evolved to make sense of direct, natural experience to this kind of mediated, unnatural experience, the models of this newly accessible reality which our minds construct become distorted and nonsensical, and we have little insight into the degree of the distortion.

When you look at a television report containing a scene in Borneo, say, it fills your mind about as much as a scene in the room in which you are sitting. You have no instinctive grasp of the magnification applied by the artificial instrument through which you are looking. Nothing tells you that you are looking at something 11 000 kilometres away which is therefore magnified four million times. And that is considering only one dimension.[31] It would be four million times *squared* if you consider two dimensions, and the magnification if you consider all the points in a *sphere* of that radius is beyond meaningful representation.

I remember once being surprised by a New York taxi driver who (a) wanted to know whether I knew Prince Charles and (b) thought that England was about as large as the USA. Clearly this man was less well equipped by nature for constructing a realistic model of his instrumentally enlarged experience than he was for driving a taxi in New York.

We do indeed live in a 'global village', with distortions which keep catching us out, as though we were in a hall of super-distorting mirrors. When we look at a scene, think about an issue or consider the importance of a threat, at all levels of magnification the view 'from where we are sitting' looks the same.

The attractive fractal patterns which illustrate books about chaos theory are an excellent illustration of this phenomenon. I have a program for my computer[32] which produces these patterns to order – for example, it will draw out the pattern of the Mandelbrot set.

Fractal patterns are the product of mathematical calculations, and by their very nature they are 'self-similar at all levels of magnification' – in other words, you can do the calculations at any level of precision, zooming in to greater and greater levels of detail, and although the pattern is different it is always just as complicated. So you get no clue about the level of magnification from the appearance of the small part you are looking at.

There is a section in the book which accompanies the program which illustrates this point. It says that Winfract allows you on your home computer to zoom in successively on a fractal ten times, each zoom magnifying the image by a maximum of about 25 times. The reader is challenged to guess (without peeping at the answer) the size that the whole of the original pattern would be by the time it has been stretched in this way by ten successive zooms. Tennis court size? A mile wide?

> *But a mile wide is the wrong answer. A Mandelbrot set blown up to the scale of the most extreme zoomed view you can see on your PC with Winfract would be* **one billion miles wide***. That is* **ten times** *the distance from the earth to the sun; almost the distance to Jupiter.*

The book shows a diagram of the solar system upon which the whole Mandelbrot set, enlarged by the same amount as you have just enlarged the fractal you can still see on your screen, is superimposed. Centred on the Sun it stretches *far beyond the orbit of Mars*.

The point is that at each level of zoom the view on the screen looks the same. And although you have carried out the zooming operation yourself, and you can see how much you are zooming and you know exactly how many times you have done it, you get *absolutely no idea* of the magnitude of what you have done. Try it. I promise you will be astonished.

I went into this matter in more detail in my book, *The Paradox of Progress*, but the point is that a doctor is just as devoid of a sense of scale when plunging into any one of the many problems of any one of the thousands of patients on his list. Similarly, a newspaper reporter is just as devoid of a sense of proportion when he is writing an article on just one aspect of public health. And the reader of a single paragraph may have just as much difficulty understanding what a tiny, but nonetheless essential, part it is of the whole idea in the author's mind.

There is another phenomenon which follows directly from this. It is that errors appear just as prominent at any level of perfection. That is a matter I shall come to in Chapter 11, on the utopian illusion.

Many a mickle . . .

My version of the old saying, 'many a mickle makes a muckle,'[33] is that adding half a minute to a long job doesn't make any difference, but adding half a minute to *every* one of a great many *short* jobs can bring life to a halt. A thousand good ideas add up to a bureaucratic nightmare.

And that is what we keep doing in the contemporary world. We are trying to do everything better all the time. And we keep making the same mistake. For example, in our health centre we keep thinking it would be more efficient to have all the reference books gathered together in a common library down the corridor – 'only half a minute away' – and then wondering why people don't use them as they used to when they could reach them from their desks. We tell each other that we all ought to make the trip more often, and we never realise how impossible it would really be to do so.

We think that the two minutes or so it takes to make a connection to the Internet are insignificant when we set them against all the benefits, but actually this is a massive block to using the web to its full potential. It oughtn't to be, perhaps, but it is. In contrast, by pressing just one button on my Compaq laptop I can have the *Oxford Compendium* (containing the *Concise Oxford Dictionary*, the *Oxford Dictionary of Quotations*, the *Oxford Dictionary of Modern Quotations* and the *Oxford Thesaurus*, all of which, in their entirety, reside permanently on the hard disk) open on the screen ready to use in four seconds flat. That is a different matter altogether. That is something I *do* use.

Time and again we dismiss the time it takes to use a tool. If the laptop is closed down, it takes half a minute to start it up, and by the time it is ready I have forgotten what I wanted to say, or if I can remember I have lost the context which made the words meaningful. You wouldn't have lasted long in the Wild West if you were as slow as that on the draw. On the other hand, I can draw my Psion from whichever pocket it happens to be spoiling at the moment, open it, press the Jotter button, and be typing a thought within three seconds. So that is something else that I really use.

However, despite this kind of practical experience, we go on making the same mistake. When you think of one job at a time, an extra bit tacked on so that you can do it better always seems justified. Especially if you are an outsider brought in to look at that bit and nothing else.

But reality is worse than this. The real killer is that progress doesn't mean just doing things better, which invariably means they take longer. It also means doing them more *often*. Whether backing up computer files, mowing the lawn, cutting the hedges in the garden or giving your patients check-ups, in all such things the essence of progress is organising yourself so that you do them more *regularly*. It is only when we try to live a life which incorporates all of these threads into what we so accurately call *real time* that we get this dreadful full-up feeling. And even then we can't really work out what is going wrong in the midst of this obvious progress, because our consciousness is not equipped to comprehend the totality of what we are trying to do.

That is the job of the subconscious, but I shall be coming to that (see p. 96). At the moment I am concentrating on the fact that our conscious minds deal with one thing at a time, which in most respects is an enormous strength, but it can be grossly misleading when we try to model the *whole*, which is reality.

The pot is getting fuller and fuller

I've had all the checks and the well-woman screening done, the smear and breast checks. But a friend had a check recently when the pulses in her feet were checked – I wonder if I could have mine done sometime?

The reality today is that everything we do is expanding outwards. We can dive into absolutely anything – references, people, contacts, hobbies – and become immersed. As I follow up chronic conditions such as high blood pressure in surgery over the years, I gently but inexorably increase the complexity of the regular checks I do. Once it would be the blood pressure and the pulse and a quick listen to the heart. Then I started checking various blood tests and the ECG, then the cholesterol, and then, inch by inch, I started doing these checks more regularly and more often. At every stage I am trying to emulate what seem like sensible things that other people are doing, as well as occasionally incorporating my own ideas.

But the truth is that success continually recedes as we (and the patients) get used to each stage. Perfection is never achievable, and the further we go towards it the steeper the path becomes. Further progress becomes ever more difficult, but since making progress is what provides so much of our motivation and satisfaction, just staying where we are becomes more and more like drudgery. One man's exciting innovation will become, a few years down the line, part of what is expected, along with all the other people's exciting innovations, which in turn will come to be expected as well. Everything is branching out in three dimensions. The wood is getting thicker and thicker, and because of our obsession with retaining records and aiming for perfection, no one is doing any pruning.

A lot of the time it is tremendous fun, but it is not working out as expected. A lot of the time it *isn't fun* and it is making people ill. There is no elbow room. There is less and less room to fly. We seem to be going more and more vertically up the wall, and we feel close to the point where we are going to drop off it backwards like exhausted mountaineers. The metaphors come racing at us – we are trying to push back the tide, we make a big effort here, we think we are making progress, then it starts slipping through somewhere else, suddenly the water seems to be all around us. Our efforts are running into the sand, like the mighty Okavango river spreading out into its gloriously fertile inland delta and then dissipating completely into the Kalahari desert. We are coming, perhaps, to the end of progress.

And now, with our newly superhuman vision, we have a view of a vast number of tiny risks, every one of which it seems essential to avoid. We are paralysed by a suddenly enhanced view of the dangers around us – ill-equipped to make sense of the distorted picture.

There is less and less to do which is new, and we use up more and more of our energy just staying where we are. At the same time we have never had so many possibilities open to us – wonderful summaries in weekend papers of all the things we can do with our spare time, so many personal contacts we should maintain. We can get to so many people with our cars and our roads. We can telephone them on the mobile, on a handy extension, sitting in the bath, on a mountain top – take your pick. We can fax them, email them and send them scans of the holiday snaps in colour and in a choice of resolutions. We can send copies of our letters and emails to lists of friends. We can desktop publish. We can print in colour. We can have dozens of computer games to play, but each of them needs weeks to learn in order to do well. Through the Internet we can 'browse' freely through 800 million publicly available web-pages (two years ago the figure was 320 million), but even this amazing system is becoming overloaded.[34] The road outside our house connects us to every place in the world, but we still cannot go to more than one of them at once. The Internet may have eliminated the travelling time, but the basic problem remains the same.

However, we *want* to go everywhere, and we *try* to go everywhere. The world still behaves as though it *expects* us to go everywhere. Managers jack-boot on to the scene and *tell* us to go everywhere. But it isn't as easy as any of us think.

We have automatic Internet tools which will email us with lists of items we have said we want to know about, but somehow the thing we want is never on the list, and the things that are on it seem predictable and dull. Life is getting full up – too many classics to keep up with, too many friends, too many photographs, too many negatives, all those wonderful holiday videos – when do we watch them?

Far too many CDs. Nobody guessed that CDs would become so cheap that we wouldn't be able to pack any more of their fat little cases on to our shelves.

The point is that all of this has to be fitted into one life, into the time in one life and into the energy in one life. And that makes life feel like a tightly stuffed pillow, about to burst – a saturated sponge. Filled with little things that appear insignificant in isolation – a gridlock of good intentions.

That is what people who are busy on the front-line feel like a lot of the time. And because the fullness is made up of little things which they can't think about all at once, they can't explain the fullness to outsiders, nor can they explain the deeper mystery, simply because they can't understand it themselves – that all those little things are not little at all on their own. The little things are the *only* things that are important in the end. That is the mystery – they are actually the *big* things. It is only when you stand back that you can no longer see it and that you can't understand the fullness.

Outsiders can't understand, for example, why it is that across so many cultures and so many generations teaching has been organised to allow teachers and learners alike regular, extended periods for mental refreshment – in other words, long holidays. Now that teaching is run by outsiders they have hit upon the idea of making teaching more efficient by minimising these outdated, unproductive intervals. They laugh at their forebears for failing to think of something so obvious, and they think how primitive they must have been.

People cope, it is machines that have the problems

> *It's the lifeboat problem. If you get too involved with too many people with too many problems they drag you under. You don't save* **them**, *they sink* **you**.
>
> Robert M Pirsig[35]

We return to the double failure of perception. Despite the fact that life is even fuller than we think it is, ordinary human beings (teachers and GPs, for example) actually cope with that fullness much better than seems possible, provided that they are allowed to get on with it. We all take the 'outsider' view as soon as we step back from the front line. I know very well that I only have to go away for a weekend to forget what the pressures of work are really like.[36] We all forget, in our role as outsiders, that the way we cope in our role on the front line is qualitatively different to the way outsiders imagine it to be. And the principal manifestation of this qualitative difference is the lack of precision and absolutism.

Watch a GP scanning a journal. If you are a GP, watch *yourself* doing it, as I have just done with this week's *BMJ* and *Lancet* over lunch in the sun. You turn the pages almost continuously, about one every two seconds, your eyes scan the headlines, the first line or two of the abstracts, the pictures and the tables. The process is largely automatic. You spot things that interest you and you keep momentarily stopping. Then you get right into something interesting and you suck out its gist, like a predatory insect.

This is not a primitive process. This is not slovenly, nor is it carelessness – this is something extraordinarily sophisticated. We have a right to take a great deal of pride in our common ability to do it.

On a plane . . .

General practice, like life, is a constant struggle to do your best in an infinitely open-ended job. GPs sense (but cannot explain) that they can never fulfil society's and their own expectations of perfection. They are enormously affected by too many pressures. As a GP you are at the mercy of chance events – symbolised by your ever-present bleep, your ever-ready phone – and all the time there is a small but real possibility that you may suddenly be thrust into a life-and-death drama in which you are a central character. It is a hugely stimulating and rewarding role, but at the same time there is a line beyond which you can become overwhelmed.

This reminds me of the way my Laser sailing dingy used to plane across the water, flying from crest to crest in an exhilarating cloud of spray – across the faces of the breaking waves in a strong, warm, onshore wind in Brittany – and that complete contrast when you drop off the plane, slow down suddenly and plough heavily into the water. The transition from loving every minute of it to feeling immersed is as sudden as it is complete.

Here is a different analogy I would like to share with you, namely that of heart failure. Normally the heart beats extremely efficiently – few things are more vital. Each time the heart relaxes, its chambers are filled with blood from the great veins. Then, when it contracts or 'beats', the inlet valves close and the blood is forced through the outlet valves into the great arteries. Pulsing through smaller and smaller arteries, the blood finds itself between the cells of the body, where it trades oxygen and nutrients such as glucose for various kinds of waste. After this it is driven up the progressively enlarging vessels of the venous tree, helped on its way by the contractions of surrounding skeletal muscles acting against one-way valves, and eventually arriving back at the heart. Round and round it goes, an endless job, like an in-tray you empty every evening before you go home, but which is always full again in the morning.

A failing heart cannot manage to keep this up. It doesn't empty the in-tray each day. Its chambers do not empty completely with each beat, a backlog builds up and the pressure in the veins rises. All night the heavy burden weighs on the subconscious mind. Fluid seeps out of the veins into the tissues around the ankles, producing the classical picture of dropsy, and pressure building up in the veins in the lungs causes fluid to accumulate there as well, compressing the air sacs and causing shortness of breath.

Treatment of heart failure involves either strengthening the heartbeat with drugs such as digitalis and ACE inhibitors, or removing excess fluid from the system so that the backlog is relieved, or both.

So it is with the overloaded human mind. Just as we take our heartbeat for granted, so we take the way in which our minds cope with complexity for granted as well. The way we cope is by compartmentalising, by dealing with things, finishing them off and moving on. But it is not easy, and we need help and understanding to do it, not more and more pressure. If you give someone in heart failure a transfusion of extra blood, however well-meaning you may be, you can kill them. It's an elementary mistake, but it happens.

The size and cost of the report you sent out concerning the recent Mental Health seminar was not matched by its content. In these pressurised times, front-line workers are becoming increasingly exasperated by massive documents of this kind. If, as seems probable, one of your seminars is about to discover the wheel, is there any way of limiting the number of forests that are cut down to bring us the news?

The situation is not hopeless. This letter brought a good-humoured, slightly embarrassed, if not actually apologetic, response when I wrote it in exasperation to a manager a year or so ago. In fact it is not us but machines that cannot cope with complexity. The more that society tries to turn us into machines, the more difficulty we have in coping ourselves. The illusions we are discussing affect the machines far more than they affect us. Reality is hidden when you are in the outsider role and you have the privilege of thinking about only one job at a time.

The difficulty of forgetting carefully

It is hard work to forget carefully. Weeding a database or indeed a filing cabinet is hard work – much harder than you think it will be. I know all too well that I am further from this particular goal at the end of my sabbatical than I was at the beginning. As we become more machine-like, we develop a kind of negative amnesia – *Remiehzla's* disease if you like.[37] We can't forget *anything*. The struggle we have to cope with our personal experience of reality is similar to the struggle society has to cope with its *collective* experience of reality. Almost every personal problem has its equivalent on the wider stage, and the clutter in the study is like the clutter in society's agenda. Selection, choosing, excluding, forgetting, disposing and recycling are becoming more and more necessary, and these are things that machines are bad at doing for us.

Increasingly, our world resembles the home of an old man with Diogenes syndrome.[38] Every nook and cranny is being stuffed with junk, the ability to throw anything away has been lost, and like him we have lost the ability to see how squalid our environment has become.

Factors in the fullness

In summary, here are some of the factors which have come together to produce the fullness we experience on the front line today.

- Technology has extended the 'reach' of our senses, but biology has given us no corresponding ability to understand by how much. We can judge the incoming flight of a ball with greater precision than any machine, but we can't get a health scare on the morning news into proportion with dangers we commonly experience at first hand.
- This increase in our experience has been accompanied by a hidden, exponential increase in the internal complexity of that experience. For example, we think that doubling the number of people in an organisation will make it twice as difficult for everybody to shake hands with everybody else, but actually it makes it *four* times as difficult. Tripling the number will make the same thing *nine* times as difficult. Increasing the number by ten times will make it a *hundred* times as difficult.
- Just as new as the increased 'reach' of our experience is our ability to *archive* our experience in permanent ways. Throughout history, mankind has sought for better ways of remembering. Suddenly we have lost the ability to *forget*, and the air about us is thick with the records of the undead past.
- Technology has given us an expectation of perfection and an intolerance of risk. Total Quality Management philosophy, revolutionary in the manufacture of defect-free goods, is now being applied to the humanities.
- Media technology focuses selectively on risks that arc remote and horrific, and blows them out of proportion to the great mass of events which appear dull and uninteresting. This distorts our perceptions of risk and threatens to bring life to a nightmarish, hypochondriacal halt.
- To the over-mind all finite risks look the same, regardless of their probability. Front-line workers are unable to protect themselves against their own vulnerability to retrospective censure. The fact that a particular risk was extremely unlikely on the human scale is no longer a defence for having failed to take known precautions against it.

Society's judgement with regard to what constitutes a reasonable level of precaution is crucially dependent on the validity of its perceptions and of its models of reality. False models create nothing less than a busybody's charter and a nightmare for people who are trying to do their best in real jobs.

The great irony of the technological age is that machines are not being used to empower people so much as to enslave them. Despite technology, people are losing control. Where people *are* empowered by technology, it is within those aspects of their lives which they control themselves, especially their leisure and their retirement. Technology only empowers them in their work when they have the good fortune to be their own bosses.

The problem is that powerful people have seized the opportunities provided by technology to impose something akin to a new form of slavery. This slavery carries sinister echoes of the 'new dark age' which was foreseen in 1940 by Winston Churchill if the Battle of Britain were lost: 'made more sinister, and perhaps more prolonged, by the lights of a perverted science'.[39]

Come, let me speak to nations on my phone,
While driving (with one hand) my sports coupé.
And let me strum my laptop, which alone
Can harmonise the threads which make my day.
And, Boeing, jet me off to distant meetings,
rub my shoulders there with divers hues.
And bring me back at night to snatch a fleeting nap;
then packaged supper; then the news.
Come Internet, come email, burst my in-tray.
Come massive Sunday paper, glossy mag.
Come rolling fax, come humble mail, have your say;
Come shouting Babel uproar none can gag.
    This tide must flood; this sanity must ebb –
    Trapped in the epicentre of this web.

CHAPTER SIX

The absolute, the new, change and entrapment

They still do it in the arm, do they?
22-year-old having his blood pressure taken

Mrs Greenfield, a new patient, is looking for something in her out-size handbag as she comes through the door to see me for the first time. As she sits down she shuffles some papers nervously on to my desk. 'Sorry, doctor,' she laughs, 'I'm a bit clumsy.'

'That's OK, don't worry.' I smile and try to put her at her ease.

Her husband, sitting down beside her, laughs and smiles as well. We all smile as she continues her search.

At last she finds what she is looking for – a paper bag. From this she draws a battered cardboard box and from this a device like an electronic calculator which, with enormous pride, she presents to me.

'Ah, you've got a Glucometer.'

'Yes, my last doctor told me to get it.'

She is obviously a diabetic . . .

To manage diabetes properly you have to look after the amount of glucose in your blood, because your body won't look after it for you. That is the problem with diabetes. That is why Glucocheck machines are such an advance.

I explain this to patients all the time, or try to, something like this. Sugar is the fuel of the body. It is carried around the body in the blood in the form of glucose, and it passes from the blood into the cells where it is burned to give you energy. And we all need energy, don't we?

Pause for weary laugh.

The glucose gets into the blood from the food in the intestine. If you eat pure glucose it can get straight into the blood, even through the lining of your mouth, but most foods have to be broken down by digestion before they can be absorbed. The oxygen which is needed to burn the glucose comes from the lungs, of course, so the bloodstream is our transport system, carrying glucose and oxygen from where they arrive in the body to where they are needed.

Now the whole point about diabetes is that glucose cannot get out of the blood without insulin. It can get in, but it can't get out. The glucose molecules are rather like souls having to wait for Charon[40] to carry them in his boat across the Styx into Purgatory.

But the lack of energy in the cells isn't really the main problem with diabetes. Most of the time the problem is that the sugar concentration in the blood gets too high and the blood vessels don't like it when the blood is too syrupy. Over a period of years, the excess sugar damages them and they start clogging up, particularly in the eyes and in the legs.

So the whole point about diabetes is that while you must have some glucose in the blood, you don't want too much. Diabetic control is all about balance. That is why the Diabetic Association calls its magazine '*Balance*'. No sugar is bad, some sugar is good, and too much sugar is bad again. As with many other things, doctors are not for or against sugar, we just want a reasonable amount.

And that is why measuring blood sugar directly is such a breakthrough. In the past the only test that diabetics could perform for themselves was to see if there was any sugar in their urine. This was second-hand information. Sugar only gets into the urine when it gets above a level that the kidneys can hold back. The body is normally good at retaining sugar – after all the trouble of finding, eating and digesting food, it would be pretty silly if you just peed it out again. So the kidneys are good at keeping sugar out of the urine. But there are limits, and if the level gets high, above what is called the 'renal threshold', some of it starts to appear in the urine. Medical students are told the story of a wise old physician who diagnosed diabetes in a show-business personality from the spatters of dried glucose on the toecaps of his patent leather shoes.

So being able to test the level of sugar in the blood directly for yourself is an example of real progress, like a speedometer to tell you that you are going too fast, instead of having to wait for the police-car to stop you. In the past, blood sugar tests were an occasional luxury because the doctor had to send a small bottle of blood away to the laboratory. But now you can just squeeze a drop of blood on to a stick impregnated with reagents, wait the right length of time and you get a colour change proportional to the sugar concentration in the blood. You can estimate the colour change by eye, but the Glucometer machine does it better, and it also does the timing. So you put in the stick, the machine counts down to zero, emits a 'beep' and there is the figure on its screen. Then you can see whether it is high, low or OK.

Well, here is Mrs Greenfield showing me her book of blood sugar results from her meter as though it is an album of photographs from her family wedding.

I take my cue, open the book and survey the columns of neatly copied numbers with an appreciative smile. Then I look at them more carefully, and see that they are not good. I look up at her, still smiling but showing a little surprise. 'These figures are high, aren't they?'

She looks utterly stunned. 'High, doctor?' Figures are figures. Do they have height?

'I'm afraid they are. Very high, actually. What are you doing about it?'

'Doing about it?' She is crestfallen.

I feel a complete heel.

Time for my lecture . . .

Singin' the blues

A Glucometer is a machine which turns a particular shade of colour (something which is obviously relative) into a figure (something which is obviously absolute). In other words, it is an analogue-to-digital converter. Analogue-to-digital converters themselves come in different shades.

At one end of the spectrum, a blue colour change is used to signal a pregnancy. That is fair enough, as a pregnancy is a famously all-or-nothing (i.e. digital) situation. Hence the joke about the girl who said she was 'just a little bit' pregnant. Nor is it too unreasonable to use the fading of special blue bristles to indicate when a toothbrush is needing replacement, I suppose. But when we use the fading of a blue stripe on our Gillette Mach 3 razor-blade to tell us that we are no longer 'getting the optimum shaving experience' (as it says on the packaging), we are descending into farce.

An experience is an experience – we don't need a signal to tell us we are getting it. We don't need a blue light on the bed-head (or more likely a red light) to tell us that we are having an optimum experience in bed. But it takes a bold shaver to carry on using a Gillette Mach 3 razor-blade when its blue stripe is as bleached as a bone in the desert, although mine goes on working fine when I do. It might just as easily be the other way round, because the factors that determine the rate at which blue dye leaches out of a strip of plastic are quite different to the ones which determine how quickly the edges of the nearby blades are dulled. However obvious this becomes when we think about it, we have an immensely strong natural inclination to treat things that are relative as absolutes, and here the advertising industry is merrily exploiting our confusion.

I was looking at the expiry date on an ampoule of diclofenac pain-killing injection from my emergency bag the other day and noticed that the expiry date was exactly two years after the date of manufacture. I mean *exactly* two years (Made: 1 June one year. Expires: 1 June two years later). Either nature was being extraordinarily helpful, or it was blindingly obvious that the expiry date was hugely arbitrary. Whoever had had the job of deciding the interval must have more or less picked the figure out of the air, allowing a generous margin of error for variations in storage temperature, and so on.

But try telling that to the patient to whom you have just given the injection, who notices that the drug 'went out of date' a week ago. Especially if he thinks it has made him feel ill (and it is in the nature of our work that we inject things into people who are likely to feel ill). With something as consequential as a medicine it is enormously difficult to justify allowing common sense to override the figure that is printed so clearly on the label. It is enormously difficult not to appear sloppy or unprofessional.

But in reality, backing your judgement in circumstances like this is the essence of professionalism. Drugs do not suddenly change into poisons on the stroke of midnight, like Cinderella's coach into a pumpkin, any more than cornflakes or strawberry jam do. We know that, but the official world we are increasingly signed up to has forgotten it, or is incapable of coping with such complexity.

OK, OK, so other things being equal, if you are restocking your bag and some drugs are past (or near) their expiry date and there are others available which are not, then obviously you choose the new ones.

But usually other things are *not* equal. You may be dealing with an emergency and the 'expired' drug is the only one available at the time, and the only alternative is not to give anything at all. What do you do then? Or you may be dealing with an expensive drug, and premature dumping of stock may waste a great deal of money which cannot then be spent on other kinds of healthcare that are perhaps more important. Another consideration is the length of the 'shelf-life' of the drug. An extra week on a demonstrably arbitrary two-year period is obviously immaterial, but an extra day on the two-day shelf-life of a fresh salad may be of great importance.

You may say that the only answer to all this complexity is to have a figure and stick to it rigidly. But the answer to *that* is that the resolving of this type of subtle complexity is exactly what the educated human mind is supremely good at doing. It is what the human mind is *for*, provided that we keep it in practice and provided that society respects the ability and allows the space which it needs to operate. At the moment, society is moving blindly away from respect for that ability, towards simplistic, rigid control by unchallengeable rules. What is worse is that it is becoming increasingly pointless for individuals to try to understand the rationale of these rules, let alone to question whether such a rationale exists.

Our minds have this extraordinary affinity for things that are fixed and absolute – things that aren't fuzzy, things that are certain. They like figures, league tables and scores. The 1999 European Cup final was being played on the evening when Lesley and I went up to London to see Michael Frayn's *Copenhagen*, which, as it happens, is all about uncertainty. We came out of the theatre to find young men shouting in the street in celebration of Manchester United's victory. It was only later that we learned that United had won by scoring two goals in injury time, their opponents having scored in the first five minutes and then dominating the game right up until those final, freakish moments. This did not affect the celebrations, the result, the cup, the memory or the history books in the slightest. And why should it? That's the way rules work.

So here again we have two completely different and mutually uncomprehending views of reality.

Entrapment

A hospital has been reported to the Health and Safety Executive after a baby was found playing with a box of syringes.
　　Fourth item on the BBC radio morning news, 7 October 1995

The more I try to make sense of the world, the more I am impressed by the way in which, in so many contexts, we find our minds drawn by fixed ideas. You can almost feel yourself being sucked into a vortex. I'm sure that this effect must have been noted before, but I am unaware of it having been given a name, and for the purposes of this book I am going to use the term *conceptual entrapment*. The name carries with it the useful connotation that we are victims of this effect, and that it might be a good idea to think about how to escape. Entrapment is another of the natural, hidden propensities of our minds, like their phenomenal powers of selectivity, which have been artificially exaggerated in the shared mind of our society.

The way the mass-media *lock on* to minor issues is an example, like the above news headline about the baby found playing with a box of syringes. We are not even talking here about *needles* – although I can't imagine any baby getting through the packaging even if it *had* been a box of needles. But even if it had done so, and had managed somehow to stab itself with a (guaranteed sterile) needle – *the fourth item on the national news . . . ?*

Surely this is the same phenomenon as ducklings imprinting on the first moving object they see after hatching from their shells, and then treating it as mother for the rest of their lives, even if it is a man.

Surely it is the same phenomenon as falling in love at first sight. Like the touching story of Catherine Boucher, on the occasion when a young engraver called William Blake entered the room when he was visiting her father. She 'instantly recognised her future partner' and 'was so near fainting that she left the room until she had recovered'.[41] After their marriage she supported him in what seems to have been a relationship of genuine mutual devotion throughout the hardships and bitter disappointments of their arduous life. Their shared faith in his genius was entirely untouched by the indifference of the world. This entrapment was no flash-in-the-pan romance – it was something wholly good.

So this phenomenon which I am calling entrapment is a human characteristic with a biological purpose which can clearly be a force for good. But I am suggesting that when it is transposed to the higher level of the common consciousness of society, it is not only exaggerated, but we lose control of it as well as our intuitive understanding of the magnitude of its power.

Hypersensitisation

It is rather like an allergic reaction. Our society's common mind becomes as hypersensitive to particular topical issues as any hayfever sufferer to a particular pollen. Ready-primed reporters roam the media-waves just as ready-primed antibodies roam our bloodstream, and when they find what they are looking for they trigger a reaction every bit as arbitrary and inappropriate, and very nearly as dangerous, as the anaphylactic reaction provoked by penicillin in an allergic subject.

At a time when the nation is highly attuned to medical scandals, for example, a surgery 'somewhere up north' warns a few patients that it may have had a problem with an instrument steriliser and, bingo, it makes the national news.[42] Meanwhile countless unfashionable issues of incomparably greater importance receive no attention whatsoever.

In writing this book I find it a constant battle to avoid becoming entrapped in whichever part I happen to be involved with at the moment. I need to keep shaking myself out of the rut and moving on to the shaping of the larger idea. Nor do I want to become entrapped in anyone else's idea of what I am trying to say. When trying to obtain approval for my study leave, I argued that I wanted to keep the whole project fluid for as long as possible, because my main purpose was to clarify in my own mind what exactly it was that I felt so strongly I needed to say. I was acutely aware of the danger that the idea could so easily crystallise *wrongly*.

I was pretty sure that this idea of entrapped ideas was near the centre of it all – to the understanding of why our society is so attracted to rigid ideas, to measurements, to plans and to protocols. And to my suggestion that the modern world's avowed espousal of rationality may itself contain a component which is profoundly *irrational* – that we may, in short, have gone overboard about it all (nor is there anything remarkable in this idea – it is what everybody thinks – they just feel inhibited about saying so out loud, especially to important people). And that is why, while I feel the lure of these things so strongly myself (I can write a protocol as tightly as anyone else), I think it is essential that at least some of us should recognise the whirlpool ahead and make an attempt to steer away from it.

The attraction of the edge

So, our minds lock on to absolutes, but they also select the new. This, like the eye being exquisitely sensitive to movement, is an efficient way of picking out the part of a scene which merits our attention. Everything from a satellite which is moving against the background of stars in the night sky, to a particular kind of localised twitching in the hawthorn hedge I can see now as I look up through my window, which tells me that a family of long-tailed tits is feeding inside it in their characteristic way.

So much of the interest lies in the movement at the edges of things. News is interesting precisely because it is new. My mother has a lifelong interest in clothes, and even in her old age she can home in unerringly on the latest fashions in a department store. All the interest in fractal patterns is at their edges, and the detail goes on for ever. It is the subtlest nuance of a musical performance that makes it exceptional and makes it moving. The devil is in the details, no doubt, but so is God.

We are wise to be wary of new illnesses, because they carry a threat which cannot be quantified. Nor can the reality of their initial threat ever be fully recaptured in retrospect.

At the time of its first appearance, the human immunodeficiency virus might, for all we knew, have been as infectious as influenza.

Similarly, bovine spongiform encephalitis might have been transmitted in milk, putting the entire human race in peril. The risk was probably very small, but of such consequence as fully to justify concern at the time.

Crops which have been genetically modified to produce insecticides in their sap may yet turn out to have unexpected consequences for ecological balance.

The wholesale replacement of traditional, self-motivated GPs in the NHS with monoclonal rule-followers may result in patients looking elsewhere for what they require in a doctor.

We are right to worry about such things. It is a profound error to look back when (or if) experience, not to mention scientific testing, has eliminated the uncertainty and think that concern at the time was foolish and that those who expressed it were 'prophets of doom'.

The problem with making back-ups of computer files is that the back-ups are all too often out of date and you are selectively interested in the things you have done recently (i.e. since the last back-up). The problem with computer virus-checkers is that although yours contains profiles of many thousands of viruses, it is the *new* viruses, the ones that would have been in the update you haven't found time to download yet, which are the *only* ones which are actually likely to give you problems.

When you walk into a bookshop you are confronted first with a display-table of *new* books. They are no better than the old ones – in fact, it stands to reason that they are likely to be worse than the old books which have survived on the shelves – but nonetheless they are the ones we look at first.

Similarly, the current issue of a magazine always has an enormous added value compared to the back issues which we doctors tend to keep in our waiting-rooms. If magazines somehow lost the colour from their covers as soon as they were no longer current, the difference could hardly be more stark or more tangible.

Funny, isn't it?

One thing is certain, nobody has to *tell* us to be interested in change.

At a journal club meeting in our health centre I once presented an article from the *BMJ* describing a simple manipulation technique which was claimed to have a high success rate in the treatment of patients with benign positional vertigo[43] – a common, distressing and relatively harmless form of giddiness which had been notoriously difficult to treat. To my surprise, I found that six of the ten doctors in the room had already seen and read the article.

Remember what I said earlier about it taking 24 hours to read one issue of the *BMJ* thoroughly? All those doctors were receiving something like a dozen journals every week, never mind all the other forms of newly written material, all the books that have been recommended as 'compulsory reading for every doctor' and all those helpful audiotapes, videos, CD-ROMs, and then of course the Internet, which gives, at least potentially, 'instant' access to the whole of knowledge.

It is a remarkable fact that despite all of this, most of my colleagues at that journal club had spotted the significance of the particular article I had chosen to present. The same thing happened more recently when I described an article about a new technique for helping people with blocked Eustachian tubes. These are the types of 'trivial' problem which are not at all trivial when you have them yourself, or when people bring them to you expecting help. Somehow our minds remain on the alert and they home in automatically – far more than we give them credit for – when we see something that may help to solve such problems, even ones we would never have thought to include on a list.

Again, something odd and counter-intuitive is going on. It is as if our minds compile a list of outstanding problems – far more extensive and far more flexible than anything we could ever create in a fixed form – and automatically keep the whole thing up to date from second to second. This would explain why 70-page protocols which committees take months to produce and then years to get round to updating (if they ever do update them in the excitement of producing *new* protocols) seem clumsy and rigid. It also casts doubt on the wisdom of compelling doctors to adhere to such protocols – like forcing ballet dancers into suits of armour, safer in a way, but missing the point.

Protocols are petrified thinking. They have important uses, but the idea that they are better than thinking, or that they have replaced it, is a deeply seductive whirlpool into which our society has been sucked.

When confronted by too many things to do, there is a great human tendency to go out, get away and do something *new*. It is so much easier to go out and buy some new clothes than sort out or even *mend* the old ones. There is the same attraction in *getting right away* on holiday. If you want to make a mark in the world, you make it by doing something new, almost never by consolidating the old or the traditional. Our society has grasped this proclivity with the utmost relish. The vast, overstuffed cushion of life is constantly being made still fuller by people pushing in their extra bit of change, making a virtue of concentrating on that bit and excluding the whole. The fact that the whole is on the point of bursting is not their problem – and certainly not, they know, their fault.

I once took wry pleasure in replying to a lavishly produced invitation to yet another course on the management of change by saying that the last course I had attended had been on 'assertiveness', and that it had taught me to say 'no'.

Games always have *rules*

It has become fashionable for people in many walks of life to describe themselves as 'players'. Bankers, businessmen, even whole corporations call themselves 'players' (or 'major players', still more impressively). Not players, I think, in Shakespeare's sense, 'All the world's a stage, and all the men and women merely players'[44]; our modern 'players' are talking about a game. And games are played according to rules which are defined, laid down, rigid and decided. Everything is either right or it is wrong. You score two goals in injury time and you have won, and that is the end of the story.

Doctors are called many things, but no one calls them players. No one calls teachers players either, except when they are actually on the stage – and strangely enough, in my experience, it tends to be doctors, teachers and nurses who actually do appear on stages. As amateurs, of course. On the other hand, the players of business 'games' seem to have no time for Shakespeare's kind of playing, except as passive spectators. But then again, Shakespeare did say 'merely' players. Although he also said 'The play's the thing', as if his kind of play was what really mattered in the end.

Funny things, words.

The name that people give to doctors and teachers is 'professionals', and that is another interestingly ambiguous area, because true doctors and true teachers are also 'amateurs' in the true sense – they do it for the love of the thing, which is the best reason in the world. Perhaps that is why they are more comfortable on the stage than the people who play the business game. Originally professional cricketers were the ones who made their living from the game. They were looked down upon by the amateurs who had other means of financial support and played only for the love of the game. Until 1968, professional tennis players were excluded from Wimbledon. Again the amateurs sought to keep themselves apart.

When businessmen stopped making 'things' and started making money

Something changed in business at about the same time that something changed in society's conception of authority. The idea took root that cutlers, for example, or shoe-makers or car-makers were no longer in business to make better knives, for example, or shoes or cars – they were in business to make *money*. If making money required making better cars, then that was a necessary step in achieving the real goal. The 'goal' of the 'game', that is.

If, on the other hand, they could make more money by finding a way of getting their product bought more often, by making it wear out immediately its guarantee period expired, by promoting regular changes of fashion, by engineering successive waves of technical obsolescence (as is achieved so spectacularly successfully in the computer industry), then that would be a better way of winning the game. In other words, achieving 'the bottom line', and we all know what is on the bottom line – money, just as it is in politics. After all the talk of high-minded issues and idealism is over, we all know what settles the election: 'It's the economy, stupid.'

Solicitors don't play God

Another series of meetings at our health centre, like the journal club, was with groups of professional colleagues from the town. One evening we met the solicitors, and I was struck by the absolute difference in ethos between our two professions. One of the things to which the solicitors wanted to draw our attention was their need for us to write medical reports as fully and impressively as possible. They wanted us to include everything we could think of, however peripheral, to support their client's case.

Our comment was something to the effect that we would only do this if we thought that the case was justified. The solicitors were appalled by this, and accused us of playing God ('playing' again). We said yes, we do play God a little. They said that they play to *rules*. To be fair they didn't call it a *game*, but their attitude clearly reflected the way counsels for the prosecution and for the defence see themselves as playing – and winning or losing – a game. And although they have personal feelings about the cases they deal with, of course, in their professional lives they are effectively amoral.

It's a big difference, and interestingly enough when we met the local clergy (perhaps the last people on earth to say that they are playing God), we had a strong feeling, certainly I did, that we had much more in common with them in the kind of job we did than we had with the solicitors.

Imagine driving safely on a wide, empty road on a Sunday morning and being caught in a cunningly laid speed-trap. The infringement of the rule is absolute and final. The fact that you were driving safely is fuzzy, a matter of opinion, and can never be certain. And while it is driving safely that is actually important, the stain on the previously unblemished record is permanent. 'Your insurance company will take a dim view,' says the well-meaning friend. You have been 'proved' to be a bad driver. Such is the dominance of the absolute.

This discussion may go some way towards explaining the visceral revulsion felt by the entire British medical profession in 1990 when the Thatcher government suddenly imposed, without consultation, a *business* ethos on the National Health Service, in place of the *service* ethos that was so proudly embodied in its very name. The NHS was nearly 50 years old, and this was the first time that its great potential weakness – that it was owned and paid for by the government, in reality acting as agents for the patients, but owned and paid for nonetheless – was ruthlessly exploited. The rules of the game were clearly defined, and there could be no argument about it: 'He who pays the piper calls the tune'.

Corporate amorality

I can't see why people are not more worried about this change in our society. Game-playing – rule-following – is a cop-out. 'Let the rules take the strain.' It is much easier to comply with the rule than to solve the problem. The patient died with their electrolytes balanced. So that was all right . . .

Business seems to have been gripped by this changed ethos because it has been persuaded that it is the only way to survive. If they won't do it, their competitors will. So that's all right . . .

We express horror and revulsion at the behaviour of prison guards, officers, soldiers, even doctors, obeying orders in wars throughout history. Yet we seem to have accepted that the employees of tobacco firms, for example, have a duty to the 'bottom line' of their corporation which is higher than their duty to the safety of their fellow human beings. The history of suppressed information about the dangers of tobacco, and cynical manipulation to maximise its sales while it was known to be the most important cause of preventable death in the world, beggars belief. But it is part of a culture which accepts that the advertising industry has no duty to truth beyond that laid down in its controlling rules. The more it pushes the boundaries, the more people think it is being clever at playing its game.

Political discussion is distorted by the new phenomenon of spin-doctoring, which appears to be nothing less than clever, highly paid, professional *lying*. Again, we are expected to discuss the to and fro of this entertaining game to the exclusion of the political issues which are at stake in the election. Cabinet ministers are quite open about the clever way in which they intend to manipulate and mislead the electorate in time for the next election. OK, we are told this sort of thing has always happened, and perhaps it has, but certainly never in the past have we been so *shameless* about it. At least we pretended to *children* that our society adhered to higher principles.

There is a department of the National Health Service Executive which reads the news and finds ways of persuading the taxpayers who employ them that bad news is good. It is called the good news unit, we are told. It sounds like bad news to me.

We live, indeed, in a world which, at the official level, has become truly amoral. Cynicism abounds, and people assume that it is the way in which everyone behaves.

But it isn't.

You are going to have to trust me again. And that's a problem if you don't believe in trust. But I know doctors and teachers, and lots of other people on the ground floor of life, who don't do things 'by the book', who don't do things because that is the rule, but instead they follow a completely different ethos, a completely different authority. Something *beyond*. Something to do with personal integrity. And personal integrity, funnily enough, is another absolute.

It seems that the further you rise above the ground floor, the further you get from this old-fashioned kind of morality. That seems to me to be a reason for society to cherish and nurture the human qualities of its front-line workers – to hold them, perhaps, just a little bit in awe. A society which believes that such qualities have been superseded as an inevitable, if regrettable, consequence of progress must, I believe, be profoundly misguided.

> *No man can serve two masters . . . Ye cannot serve God and Mammon.*[45]

Old-fashioned stuff, none more so, but it is still true. The dichotomy is absolute. Nobody talks about a doctor being a 'player' – yet.

Shall I reduce your illness to a sum
– a single figure written on a screen
and tell you, 'bring it with you when you come?'
Is that, dear Mrs Greenfield, what I mean?
And shall we have a book to write it down,
for you to keep correct and up to date,
And shall I make you worry that I'll frown
The moment you exceed some going rate?
Is this the proper answer to your plea
to have a little help with your disease?
Can it be true you really came to me,
for cure by mathematical degrees?
 I think you came for something rather more –
 I think you wanted meaning, not a score.

CHAPTER SEVEN

Elbowing into the spotlight (of shared experience)

'Look, [26-year-old son] must have been my first baby after I got here . . .'

'You were with me when he was born, his second name is James.'

'We must remember that.'

'Yes, we must.'

Our muddled attitude to the classics

Holidaying in Mixtow, a tiny hamlet on the Fowey estuary, deep in the lush south-west rain-coast of England, we keep encountering the rich associations of the place. We pass Daphne du Maurier's cottage in Readymoney Cove at the beginning of a walk around the headland from Fowey, and a few miles further on the guidebook is pointing out the house where the great authoress died.

We are renting self-catering accommodation in part of Kit's house which, under its original name of 'Rosebank', was the setting for Sir Arthur Quiller-Couch's once famous novel, *The Astonishing History of Troy Town*.[46] The house was owned by his friend Edward Atkinson, who in turn inspired another friend, Kenneth Grahame, to write *The Wind in the Willows*. Atkinson ('Atky') was the prototype for Ratty and Quiller-Couch ('Q') was probably Badger. The first chapter, 'The River Bank', was written after a boating trip they made up the Fowey river 'to a little village called Golant, on the right bank, for tea'.[47] Which is uncannily like what we have just been doing. Except that we made the trip for a pub supper instead of tea, we sailed (and motored back because the wind had dropped) whereas they rowed, and, rather oddly, the little village of Golant that *we* went to was quite clearly on the *left*-hand side of the river.

Quiller-Couch was a new name to me when I first went to Fowey, but there are memorials to him all over the place, and my parents-in-law, visiting us while we were there on that occasion, recognised him immediately as one of the great literary figures of their youth. With 100 000 new books being published every year in the UK alone today, I couldn't help wondering how much longer any of these associations were going to mean anything to any of us, and whether it mattered – in anything more than a sentimental way, that is.

Yes, Daphne du Maurier's books are good, Lesley got herself a copy of *The House on the Strand* and finished it a few days after we got home, so we can agree about that. But are they *that* good? Is there something about them which makes them *absolutely* different from, better than and in a different class to the hundreds of thousands of novels that must have appeared and then disappeared into obscurity during the time they have been enjoying this label of 'classic'?

Or is becoming a classic another entrapment – a chance phenomenon of a book achieving a critical mass in the over-mind, taking it beyond what Malcolm Gladwell calls the Tipping Point,[48] after which success feeds on its success? Would it be possible, I wonder, for a really *bad* book to fulfil this role of classic?

This is the type of question which remains a question in our advanced, sorted out, analytical world, I believe, for the simple reason that it doesn't have a simple answer. But if I were to venture a simple answer, it would be 'Yes'.

Deep-seated illusions in all of our minds

One of the meetings I have attended during my sabbatical was the Medicine and Literature conference organised to celebrate the 400th anniversary of the Royal College of Physicians and Surgeons of Glasgow. The editor of the *Lancet*, Richard Horton, spoke on the Friday morning on the need for a medical 'canon' – an agreed list of medical classics.

He followed Michael O'Donnell, the distinguished medical journalist, and Richard Smith, the editor of the *BMJ*, and it was a classic morning in what was some of the hottest Glaswegian sun in the whole of the 400 years we were celebrating.

I was primed to be interested in the 'canon' idea because so much of the conversation between people attending the conference had been leaving me feeling shamefully out of touch with contemporary literature. Much of the common ground that others seemed to be sharing was unknown to me, and I felt excluded and inadequate. Silly, perhaps, but there we are.

It was just like the feeling every GP gets that he can never keep on top of all the medical literature. Perhaps, I thought, the answer was indeed for there to be a list of 'good books' for us all to go out and read so that we could chat about them in a nice, civilised way. As people do with Jane Austen – you just have to say that someone is 'a bit of an Emma', and half the world knows what you mean. And if they don't, they can go and look up the book and find out.

Half the world? As a medical student I once took a Russian student home to Oxford for the weekend on the back of my Lambretta motor-scooter. He was a big, solid chap, with halting English, and he had the reserved manner you might expect of the kind of Russian who had been given security clearance to study in Britain at the height of the Cold War. But there was a special reason why he wanted to see Oxford and the Thames – it was because he had read Jerome K Jerome's book, *Three Men in a Boat*, which is all about a boat trip up the Thames (as most readers will know – my point again).

Yes, he said, they all read *Three Men in a Boat* in Russia. It was a classic. It was humorous. We relived some of the funny bits together, and his great smile came out like the sun. The frost melted and there seemed to be hope for the world.

Richard Horton, editor of the *Lancet*, kicked off at the Glasgow meeting by telling us about a list of 200 novels written since 1950 that someone had decided everybody ought to read.[49] He said it had produced a storm of indignation. Some people thought it included books it ought not to have included, and other people thought it did not include books that it ought to have included. There was no health in it. Then he said that he had to admit that he had read less than 20% of the books in the list himself, and that while he knew of people who claimed to have read as many as half of them, he didn't believe them.

Just a moment, I thought, this is supposed to be a list of books we are all going to have in common.

Then he went on to say that he thought people ought to construct their *own* personal canons – lists of books they had liked, with reasons – so that they could recommend them to other people.

But just another moment, I thought, that is a splendid idea, I can see myself doing that, but isn't that completely missing the point of what a canon is supposed to be *for?*

It seemed to me – and my confidence had been restored considerably by the fact that my own book, *The Paradox of Progress*, had to my utter astonishment appeared at the top of the first slide of the first address of the conference on a list of (good, I think) medical literature – that he was completely failing to address the central question raised by his topic.

Surely, I thought, the idea that we can, or even should, all read a 'canon' of books and hold it in common is an *illusion*. The thing is impossible. Even if it was a practical idea to make a static list in any case. The whole thing is in a state of dynamic flux, with individual people much more interested in exploring the edges than the centre. The idea doesn't take any account of human nature – make a list of books you *ought* to read, and people will immediately find a thousand reasons for reading something else.

Canons are living things, undefinable

Richard Horton's confusion about the role of the classics is one which we all share. Every critic who reads a book and says it is 'compulsory reading' or 'should be on every bookshelf' really thinks he means what he says. He is so impressed by the book he has just been reading that he really believes his advice to be entirely justified and rational. But actually what he says so glibly, and the fact that we tend to accept it, is due to an illusion produced by the way in which our minds operate.

Because we impute to the over-mind the strengths we take for granted in our own minds, we make the mistake of thinking that something contributed to the world's literature, something that has been *published*, has necessarily been *noticed* by the world-mind (i.e. added to the world's accumulating store of experience). This is wrong. Nobody reads everything, and some things hardly get read by anybody. Gregor Mendel's papers describing the experiments which formed the basis of modern genetics were only uncovered by chance long after his death.[50] There is simply no equivalent in the artificial over-mind of society to the extraordinary capacity of the individual human mind to spot the significant detail in a mass of data (*see* pp. 69–70).

It is the same illusion that *recording* a fact in a notebook, or a data-base or somewhere in our computer means that we will thereafter be able to find it again. As the years go by and as we continue to record such facts, however cleverly we do so, the complexity will eventually overwhelm *any* system.

As a trainee GP years ago I was impressed by a lecturer who care-fully filed all his old copies of the *Lancet* and *BMJ* with articles he was interested in highlighted on the cover. They were all neatly arranged on the shelves in his study. To this day I picture those neat rows of journals and feel that I really *ought* to organise my references like that. But really I know that it is impossible.

As time goes by I develop all sorts of new and better ways of stor-ing references, each one occupying centre-stage in my mind during the time it is new, but the whole system becomes less useful as it becomes more complex. I haven't quite reached the point of throw-ing the whole lot away and starting again (like the taxi driver who said that the only answer to the congestion grid-locking the streets of New York was to concrete the whole lot over and start again on top), but there is a missing feature in all of these clever systems. None of them knows how to *forget carefully* – the thing that our own minds do so effortlessly and so automatically.[51]

The second thing that we take for granted about our minds is equally important. We assume that the publication of a book is ana-logous to the passing of a new piece of information through our minds, and we make the false assumption, because the cleverest parts of our minds operate automatically and unconsciously, that something very remarkable is being done to that new data. For our minds do not remember all the information that passes through them. They do something much cleverer and more useful than that, they compare it *all* – not just the part that reaches consciousness – with the model of the world they hold inside, and check that it fits.

To take Karl Popper's example, because it is difficult to think of a better one, a mind which believes that all swans are white will be permanently changed – and changed *without fail* – by a single, convincing sighting of one swan that is black.

But my point is that a book is different. A book, published in a world that believes all swans are white, containing incontrovertible evidence that some swans are black, may remain entirely unnoticed. And the world may sail on in ignorance of the truth.

The Internet bubble

We make all of these assumptions, most recently and most tellingly, about the Internet. The Internet is another powerful illustration of the way we impute the characteristics of our own minds to machines. We treat the Internet as though it is a super-mind.

In the scramble to 'get on the web', to put journals on-line, to have a practice website or a personal home page, which I have joined with great enthusiasm myself,[52] there is an underlying assumption that the information so presented automatically becomes part of some larger, shared experience. Time and again we see the exhortation to 'check out this site *regularly*', while we really know that there are millions of sites which are equally accessible and quite possibly more important. Yes, you *could* see any of them. No, you can't see *all* of them. It's an example of what we might call the *could-do/do-do* dichotomy. If all those sites were in a *real* mind, you would be able to see any one of them, and they would all still interact. It's a big difference.

This doesn't stop the Internet being useful and revolutionary – of course it is – but as yet we only have a simplistic view of what is new about it, and what its use will be. The striking thing about the Internet is its astonishing ability to search and *exclude*. The idea that it is some kind of integrated super-intelligence is an illusion. Any integration that goes on is going to remain, certainly for the time being, overwhelmingly within the minds of its users. In so far as our experience really is now combined into a single, global mind, the impact that each of us can make – the chance of our website hitting the jackpot and registering as a 'classic' – is smaller than before, not larger as it seems to be. The sea is now larger and each of us has inevitably become a proportionately smaller fish.

Attention-seeking behaviour

The factors that determine which voices get listened to are of crucial importance. We must examine our assumption that our society is more rational and less arbitrary in this respect than those which preceded it.

So many of the devices of information technology, from personal communication aids to advertising techniques, simply amount to new ways of elbowing your way to the front of the queue for someone else's attention. Attention-seeking behaviour in babies can vary from winning little smiles to screaming and breath-holding to the point of unconsciousness. As we get older, most of us become more sophisticated than this, but gaining attention remains a crucial factor in winning the game of life.

At the moment, huge resources are being poured into connecting doctors in the NHS to the Internet and giving them the means to send emails to one another. It is difficult to express any doubts about this, even if you are a proven techno-freak, as I am, without being dismissed as a dinosaur. But it is hard to believe that emails will ever match the crucial advantage of the telephone in actually forcing a shared moment of focused attention. The same applies to meetings, when groups of people agree to book time in one another's attention.

This exclusive use of a period of another person's finite time is a privilege which should not be abused. Otherwise we find ourselves using our computer whilst speaking on the phone, and we get reluctant meeting-draftees playing buzz-word bingo.[53] The idea that new technology can change this situation is false. The torrent of potential information is still going to have to squeeze through the mind in single file. It is the new that gets the attention, and it always will be. When faxes were new they were quite literally brought individually to your desk by running feet. When email was new we checked it eagerly several times a day. Some people are already finding that the real treat in communication today, which goes straight to the top of their priorities because it is so new and unusual, is a hand-written letter.

As for canons of shared literature, the lesson is that they will always exist in society. But they will emerge, shimmer and change for all sorts of subtle and arbitrary reasons. They will be living things. Attempts to direct them from the centre will never succeed.

While we persist in our belief that there 'ought' to be a canon of shared literature, perhaps that doctors 'ought' to read the ongoing correspondence in the *BMJ*, or the *Times* newspaper, or whatever, we are colluding with a nonsense. Now, more than ever before, it isn't going to happen, our attention is finite and it has never been so over-subscribed. The nonsense carries the implication that there is a corpus of shared understanding which has been reached in a rational and definitive way by society, and this gives the voice of the over-mind, of the media, of government and of management a spurious authority.

The joy of communicating: making a personal contribution to the shared experience

One of the principal urges in life is to communicate with people, to be significant with them and to get responses from them. Sometimes one only feels fully alive by virtue of reflections bouncing back from other people. The richest and most rewarding experiences of life involve sharing feelings with others, and the best of all involve sharing them with one person.

We are essentially tribal creatures, and we have a powerful urge to contribute to the common experience of the tribe. The classics are nothing less than the shared experience of our tribe, fulfilling the same role as the shared traditions, stories, poems, songs and myths – of a complexity almost inconceivable to us today – which were handed down through unnumbered generations before the invention of writing (or, for that matter, numbering, which is why the generations were unnumbered).

One of the reasons why even the editor of a world-leading medical journal is so muddled about the role of the classics is that none of us have thought through the implications of the way in which we are now trying to record the whole of this shared experience on permanent media, of its universal availability, and of its extension from the tribal to the global scale. Again, the view as we see it looks very much as it did when we were dealing with an oral tradition and a much more local scale. We can't grasp intuitively the scale of the change we have brought about.

We go on clinging to the idea that we still live in a tribe, or at least that we ought to. That we still live in Ambridge, perhaps, the setting of *The Archers*, or any of the other radio or television soap operas which are so immensely popular. They each have a nice, manageable couple of dozen characters, everyone knowing everyone else – one-to-one communication.

Small town life

You might think that being a doctor in a small town is like that, but it isn't. The population of Alton is 16 000, not a couple of dozen. Bring in the surrounding area and you are up to 25 000. Of those, just over 3000 are patients in our small, personal practice, and from time to time I come across a large proportion of the rest, or members of the families of the rest, whilst doing my share of the out-of-hours rota. Then include all the patients I have known over 25 years of working here – selectively concentrating on the ser-iously ill, of course, because that's what doctors do – so that the town for me is full of ghosts. Every street has a hundred stories if I let them come out of their boxes in my mind. I have lost at least a 1000 patients over the years, each of whom I have got to know really well during their final illnesses.

It's all there when something happens to make me remember. Someone reminds me of her old mum, 'Yes of course I remember, along Spitalfields Road, wasn't it?' (you always remember people first by their addresses, that's one reason why visiting them at home is so important). It's coming back now – can't show the daughter I'd forgotten, she wouldn't understand. Can't understand it myself, so why should she? Anyway, I haven't forgotten. Of course I haven't. The memory's there now, out of its box, flooding out. Vivid as yesterday...'

Going over the road

'When you come back I may be gone.'

I point my finger at the sky and raise my eyebrows.

She throws back her head and laughs in derision: 'Yeeearh.' The cigarette-stained walls reverberate with her cackling and coughing and she mops wet tears from her compound wrinkles: 'Cheeky monkey. It's a good job I don't take any notice of you.'

I'm only kidding her of course. I know perfectly well what she means is that if by some extraordinary chance I ever get round to visiting her again after my holiday, she may be down the road with her daughter for her annual change of scene.

But she's so often talking about her imminent final journey to the conveniently situated cemetery 'over the road' that I can't resist the joke. I know her sense of humour well. I am on one of the 87 visits recorded in her records leading towards the one that will say '13.10.95 Found dead in bed this morning. Very peaceful'.

Oh yes, we shared a lot of laughs:

'How long before I'm gone?'

'Well, I think you've got time to finish your tea. I might die before you do actually. Would you come to my funeral?'

'I don't think I could walk down to St Lawrence's.'

And such tea – still disgustingly strong even since I persuaded her that adding condensed milk wasn't my idea of a treat. Now she presses glacier mints on me instead.

At the age of 84 years she gave me a huge bundle of carnations from her garden to take home for my wife. Like all council houses[54] built between the wars, hers had a large garden from which she used to feed her invalid father and then her invalid husband (I can remember *him* well, too, now I think of it). Left alone after both of them had died, she went on digging it by hand and planting anything she liked in chaotic and joyful juxtaposition. She liked carnations.

And roses. I once admired the flourishing hybrid teas and floribundas punctuating her vegetables and discovered that she had propagated them all herself by cutting bits off anything she liked and pushing them into the ground. Eager to learn from such an expert (because bits we cut off things don't do that in *our* garden), I took out my notebook and poised my pen: 'Do you plant them at any particular time?'

'Yeeearh. I sticks 'em in any when. I stops when I can't go on no more.'

I wrote down her words anyway, thinking that they might be useful sometime. Some when.

She got tired of life towards the end. She started getting heart failure and I had to admit her to our community ward. After discharge she coped much better than we had thought possible, thanks to some changes in her medication, her Meals-on-Wheels[55] and her ever devoted (but also ageing) daughter. But she didn't share our appreciation of the achievement. My entry in her notes for 4 September on the year she died just said, 'Well, what'd y'want to bring me back for?' and for 6 October, when I started her on an antidepressant, 'Keeps crying. Not eating.'

I recorded 87 visits to her during the 12 years that followed her husband's death. Allowing for a few more when I didn't have the notes, it still averaged less than one a month. Not a huge effort, and pretty trivial stuff, you may think. But an incredible privilege.

21.1.94 (age 88) Dug over a flower-bed this morning.

17.2.94 ISQ[56] Smoking like a chimney.

18.3.94 ISQ 'I don't believe what you tells me.' 'The only thing that's wrong with me is I can't get on a chair' (to clean the pictures on the walls).

19.5.94 'At last' (you've come). 'Oh dear, I can't wait to get over the road.'

Come on. Snap out of it. Can't indulge like that. Can't follow up all the stories, chase all the links. You'd be overwhelmed, and never get on with anything.

It makes you feel giddy, sometimes literally, when the 'forgotten' memories of a face, a person, all the feelings, the smell of the house, the anxiety about something that wasn't right, surface again. What was it ...? Something about the family...? It usually is. The huge sagas (some of these patients have records of 200 separate consultations in their notes) come crowding out of the deep. Drawn up from that well of experience, normally hidden from sight, all of which has shaped us. Such a weight. Even just a little part of it.

A deliberate comparison between mental archives and mechanical archives

There is never any harm in explaining exactly what I am doing. Here I am making a deliberate comparison between the memory archives in our minds and the memory archives of society. Both are so much larger than we think they are. The comparison with the memory archive of a doctor is particularly interesting, because a large part of the memory of a doctor is supplemented, doubled, fixed or verified, if you like, by a carefully organised and carefully preserved written record of the same series of events,[57] providing a kind of map of what lies within one substantial area of your personal experience.

My suggestion is that the archives in our own minds are not only vaster by far than we give ourselves credit for, but that they are also managed in a way which is enormously more subtle, sophisticated, and in important ways more useful, more practical and ultimately more valid than the artificially selected and artificially stored shared experience of society which supplements them. I am suggesting that the shared records of society, including its store of classical literature, are in many ways primitive in comparison, and should be used to serve our minds, rather than our minds being made to feel that they 'ought' to serve it.

Just as we ignore all but an infinitesimal proportion of the data which is continuously being collected by our senses and monitored by our subconscious, so an even more infinitesimal proportion of the events going on in the world at large is picked out by the laser-thin spotlight of the world's attention. And just as we quickly forget all but a small proportion of the observations which *make it* into our personal consciousness, so society can only add a minute proportion of the tiny proportion of events that make the 'news', or the tinier proportion still that make the *headlines* of the news, to the longer-term heritage of commonly held ideas. And just as the information in our conscious minds is outweighed by many orders of magnitude by the amount of information in our unconscious minds, so the information held in the readily accessible over-mind of society is outweighed by even *more* orders of magnitude by the vast archives of information hidden away in less accessible forms.

It is of central importance for us to know about the factors which determine the information which emerges from this filtering process and which becomes part of our group experience, and to know whether that selection is legitimate.

For example, are 'classics' necessarily classics because they are 'best'? No, inescapably they are classics because they are classics. The hundreds of thousands of books that are not classics (that's you and me, folks, we are the 'books' in low places, just to remind you of the comparison I'm making) contain among them countless titles that many people would think as good as or better than the acknowledged classics. It is a fairly safe guess that *every* book that has ever been written would find at least one enthusiast who would claim that it was their favourite book of all.

We live in an age that is irrationally obsessed by 'celebrities'. Children grow up wanting to be 'famous'. We talk about people making their mark on the world, making their name. We 'drop names' of 'well-known' people. We want to make it to the top. We want to climb. We want to be the Olympic champion. We want to be the best. To have come second in the world is to have lost. And being best, of course, is absolute.

It is a curious irony that we have never had so clear a view of the outer world. We know far more about the personal habits and even genital peculiarities of 'celebrities' than we do about those of people we meet in our daily lives. Each one of us appears to have a seat right next to the stage.

But it is only a *virtual* seat. While the stage has never seemed closer, in reality it has never been further away, or less accessible. Actually we can see that perfectly well, too, but this does not lessen the illusion that we *could* participate. Whenever a finite possibility exists, we seem to remain curiously oblivious to how extremely small it may be. Its apparent size is more in proportion to the size of the prize, especially when the prize is large, than the chance. This applies even when the chance is smaller than almost any other finite possibility we can imagine – a fact exploited by lotteries the world over.

The point is not that this doesn't enhance life in many ways – it certainly does. It may well be that we cope with our own insignificance by identifying with significant people. But it has the effect of demeaning ordinary life and ordinary achievement, which is spurious, unfair, illogical and profoundly damaging. In the age of records, authors seeking classic status are competing with all the authors who have ever written, athletes going for records are competing with all the athletes who have ever lived, and it is closer and closer to impossible for even the best performers of the day to oust the top-ranked recordings of particular pieces of music.

So where does that leave us all in our unimaginably ordinary lives? Not too badly off at all, as it happens . . .

Celebrities actually provide very suspect role models for young people. I recently saw it pointed out that there is not a single stable nuclear family in any of the soap operas currently on UK television, and very few among the Royal Family. This matters if you believe in stable nuclear families, as I do. On the other hand, there are a large number of stable nuclear families within my personal experience, not least my own (*so far* – like being a safe doctor, or a good driver, it must always be 'so far'), and contrary to the common assumption, not all of them by any means are dull.

Giving people the idea that they can make a difference

As I write this book I am acutely conscious of how motivating it is to think that there is a chance that I might make a difference to the world, however remote that chance may be. That's what keeps me here fiddling with these words when it is sunny outside and there is a boat sitting on the drive on its trailer.

We should not underestimate the importance of giving people the idea that they could make a difference – the importance of respecting the abilities and the potential of ordinary people, ordinary writers, ordinary craftsmen. We think proudly that we have replaced traditional hereditary *authority* – aristocracy – with something we call meritocracy. But in reality both systems, the old and the new, depend largely on chance. Both, in truth, might better be described as *accidocracies*. This is not a point of view which appeals to those individuals who have been born into or achieved authority, respectively, in either system.

The standard of debate in our health centre lunch-time meetings often seems to be superior to that at conferences at national level. And so perhaps it is. When you and I think we have just as good ideas about certain issues as the people who are running the world, perhaps we are right. The fact that there have to be people in charge in the world does not automatically mean that they must be better people than everyone else. Still less does it mean that they must be the *best* people.

People in authority dominate because they are in authority. They get stuck, and we get stuck with them – another entrapment.

They are sometimes good and admirable people, but when they are not it takes a great deal to displace them. The people who pontificate from on high about the standards of teachers sometimes seem to have lower standards of their own than any teachers I know, and I know a lot of teachers well. Nor is it to diminish in the least the good *headteachers* I know to say that some of the best *ordinary* teachers I know have no interest whatsoever in becoming headteachers themselves. No, not even for the money.

'Celebrities' such as Rupert Murdoch appear to have an insatiable need to dominate the world, and appear to assume that everyone else is trying to do the same thing and therefore must be less clever and less able than they are. 'If that's their idea' (as WS Gilbert said in his opening chorus of *The Mikado*), 'they're wrong.' The best people I know are not the slightest bit interested in playing the game such tycoons think they have won against the rest of us. The taunt 'If you're so clever, why ain't you rich?' merely sums up the shallowness and emptiness of the 1980s.

The impression that life is what happens on the media stage is an illusion. It happens *here*. It happens to each of us on equal terms, as in the ancient Hindu saying 'Life is like riding an ox to find an ox'. I have never ridden an ox, but I imagine it must be a pretty overwhelming sensory experience when one does so. Therefore I think the saying means that the thing you are looking for is all around you.

It seems funny. You think and collect ideas for years, then you sit down to express them and end up telling a little story. A 'classic' story if you are very, very lucky and a critical mass of people starts to talk about it. But it doesn't seem, perhaps, quite as funny as it once did – story-telling is becoming respectable. There has been a series on narrative-based medicine (as opposed to evidence-based medicine) in the *BMJ* this year,[58] and one of the other speakers at the Glasgow conference, Bruce Charlton, gave a powerful argument for the validity of the single-case, narrative study in medical research.

And the choice of story that you are going to tell is much less arbitrary than the mechanism in society that decides which books will emerge as classics. Your mind selects (from far more candidate stories than you can ever realise) the one story that best fits the idea that you are trying to express. What is more, it automatically chooses the best story to match the audience you are addressing. Just as you subtly change your explanation of medical problems for different patients in surgery – although you joke about 'playing a tape', you never do play a tape. (In fact, playing tapes to patients has proved to be nothing like as helpful as many of us expected when the technology was new.)

So the simple story is chosen because it fits with a far from simple idea, and it is chosen in order to try to reconstruct the idea in another mind which contains a different, also far from simple, context of ideas. The story is nothing without all that background context. That is what gives it its meaning, validity and authority. To do this you just have to step back and trust your mind to do the work, just as society has to step back and trust people to do *their* work. Then you have to wait and see whether it has hit the spot. Most of the time it won't have done. The diagnosis of success – of family stability, of classic status – can only be made in retrospect. Here is something I once wrote for my weekly column *Then and Now* in *Doctor* magazine.

As usual she takes ages to come to the door. I walk round and check the back is locked (no deer in the garden today) and then resume my rat-tat-tat on the old knocker at the front, looking up at her window. Just as I am deciding to give up, the changing light through the glass panel signals movement inside. The door opens a little and she peers out. She seems pleased to see me and ushers me into the sitting-room, spotless and perfectly ordered but curiously bare where the travelling antique dealer has taken so many of the nice things I remember.

'Are you all right?'

'Oh, I'm fine, thank you.'

'They asked me to call because you couldn't walk at the day unit yesterday.'

She looks blank.

'Do you remember you go to the day unit?'

She frowns. Yes, she does remember she goes somewhere. She tries to remember its name, looking troubled, so I don't pursue it.

Sitting on her sofa I notice my old chronic-visiting summary card on the front of her notes, completed ten years ago when I visited all my over-75s and worked out my dependency scores for my two *BMJ* papers on the subject.[59] I see 'Cheerful mental state' is still ticked – hopelessly out of date now – so I alter it to 'Depressed or pleasantly confused'. Under my system that would have raised her dependency score by 5 points, and I would have increased her visiting frequency accordingly. These visits were taken over by the community psychiatric nurses long ago, of course, and I haven't seen her myself for nearly a year. Last time I was there, soon after it had been decided to try her back at home from the psychogeriatric ward, I wrote, 'Happy at home, loves her garden and the deer'.

In the hall as I am leaving I say, 'Your home is like a new pin. Do you use that hoover yourself?'

'Oh yes.' She is delighted. 'Have you been here before?'

'Yes, I used to come here quite a lot, once upon a time.'

She smiles and nods, 'Yes I remember. You're very nice.' She snuggles up to my arm.

'I'll come and see you again.'

'I'll take you up on that.'

Then on the doorstep I say, 'That *Magnolia stellata* is beautiful, isn't it?'

And suddenly she is her old self again, her face lit up with pride as she looks towards the shrub, majestic above the waist-high grass, 'Yes, they are magnificent, aren't they?'

We admire it together and I get into the car. She bends down to say something and I wind down the window to hear.

'Have you been here before?'

'Yes, I have.'

She smiles knowingly. 'Oh, because I thought perhaps you hadn't seen me before.'

We wave to each other and she closes the door happily. I stop at the top of the drive and note down her words before they evaporate.

No. Not 'raging against the dying of the light', this one. Whatever Dylan Thomas may have thought. Much more a case of 'going gently into that good night'. And thank God for that.

There's part of us thinks classics are a bore
would rather read a comic book instead;
would leave the Dickens in its upper drawer,
And hasn't time for poets who are dead.
But classic phrases 'slip beneath our guard'
Unwittingly we 'take the lines on board',
We find them 'rooted in our own backyard';
Such resonances strike a spinal cord.
And each of us would love to have the wit
To mark the world, just once, before we go.
Each bathroom-singer yearns to make a hit;
The grimmest reaper aches his seed to sow.
    But wisdom puts our feet back on the ground,
    And points to long-sought treasures all around.

CHAPTER EIGHT

Heralds of a new enlightenment

*'I don't think we were **meant** to understand . . .'*
*'Well, if we weren't **meant** to we're not doing too badly.'*

Some recent books

Hare Brain Tortoise Mind, Guy Claxton

What do you think – if you take the trouble to describe in words a face you see in a photograph, will it make you better or worse at recognising the face again?

Wrong, it will make you *worse*, a lot worse. Surprising, isn't it?

Jonathan Schooler and his colleagues did the research[60] and Guy Claxton tells us about it in his book, *Hare Brain Tortoise Mind*.[61] Claxton is an academic psychologist at Bristol University who has the knack of describing research into the way the mind functions in ways which make it easy to understand. This is how he describes this particular experiment:

> *Schooler gave subjects photographs of unfamiliar faces to study, and asked them to attempt to describe some of the faces but not others. These pictures were then mixed up with some new ones of rather similar-looking people, and the subjects were asked to pick out the ones they had seen before. The faces that had been described were recognised about half as well as those that had not, and this impairment was unrelated to how detailed or accurate a particular description had actually been . . .*

Of all the new pieces of information I have come across in my study leave, this is the one I tell people about with the most excitement. If you look at photographs of faces, you will recognise them about *twice* as accurately subsequently if you *haven't* described them in words. Wow – exactly the opposite of what you would expect, and exactly the opposite of what is *supposed* to happen.

And yet exactly the kind of thing that you can see happening if you just let yourself believe in the validity of your own experience of life, and stop listening to the experts who think they know that it *can't* happen because it doesn't happen like that in their models. Exactly the sort of thing I am trying to say in this project (i.e. listen to the reality, not to the model – reality is real, models are models). They may be useful, but they are always to some extent wrong. Sometimes they are *very* wrong.

Here, at last, after all my years of frustration with the rigidity of official ideas about postgraduate medical education[62] (and it is symptomatic of the malaise that the official world talks about 'training', not 'education'), we have experimental evidence to support my long-held belief that all of this analysing and defining of subtle things like medical judgement actually can do *harm*. That we produce good doctors in spite of it, not because of it, and that our success in doing this kind of *wrong thing* better and better is one of the things that is making so many *real things* worse. Here is Claxton's explanation:

> *The effort to describe a face so narrows our attention, and biases it towards the little that can be said, that memory is reduced quite severely.*

He goes on to give example after example of experiments and observations which show different aspects of the hidden power of what he calls the *under-mind* – in other words, the subconscious. This includes evidence that we really do sort things out when we 'sleep on them', that we really do operate better if we take a side-step and switch off our focused, logical, analytical, conscious approach for some of the time. And not just a bit better – we operate a *lot* better.

The implications for the modern world – which, as Claxton emphasises again and again, almost entirely discounts these automatic, primitive, forgotten, yet immensely powerful and sophisticated abilities within each and every one of us – are staggering.

When the significance first sank in and I realised how much they confirmed the naive, empirical observations which have for so long been at the heart of my thesis, I really did momentarily stagger. Not only did it confirm my naive, empirical observations, but it actually confirmed the *validity* of naive, empirical observations in general.

Going round in my circle again, staggering a little, but getting somewhere at last.

The friend who recommended *Hare Brain Tortoise Mind* covered himself a little. In his email he said that it was 'worth looking at, quite a light read'. The cover gives it the label of 'popular science'. I am deeply grateful to my friend for the recommendation. I am delighted if the book is popular, and I am delighted if it is easy to read, as both of these aspects enhance the book for me (if not for some academics, who sometimes seem to vie with each other to understand books which are hard to read), but the really important thing is that it should be true.

And there is every reason to believe that it *is* true, it is fully referenced and internally coherent. The fact remains that I have yet to meet one other person who has heard of it, let alone read it, so it is certainly not a classic. Not yet, despite the fact that it contains more new and important ideas, in my opinion, than Richard Dawkins' recent books (the useful central image of *Climbing Mount Improbable*[63] notwithstanding), which are read by so many people.

Wired Life, Charles Jonscher

I first read a preview of *Wired Life*[64] in the *Observer*. The author trained in electrical sciences at Cambridge and teaches information technology at Harvard, as well as running an investment firm in Europe. His subtitle is 'Who are we in the digital age?', and Will Hutton, editor of the *Observer* newspaper and himself a distinguished commentator on contemporary affairs, gives the cover recommendation:

> *Jonscher maps both the opportunities and the limits of the wired society, in the process reasserting the ingenuity and centrality of human intelligence to our future.*

Sounds like what I'm trying to say. So I get it and read it, carefully.

One lovely picture, entirely new to me, I get straight away. 'Digital' means digits – digits are fingers. Simple as that. We count on our fingers – not in our minds.

If our minds had evolved for counting, says Jonscher, we would expect them to do it extremely well. He shows just how much processing hardware our minds have available – 100 000 million neurones for a start, each one sending out connections as far as a million times the width of its own body. And not just a few connections either – each neurone makes direct connections with as many as *80 000* others.

So one thing is immediately clear. A digital computer of this size and this complexity would not stumble over double-figure arithmetic. So that, clearly and extremely significantly, is not what our minds are *for*. They are machines of a completely different kind. Not laughably bad *digital* machines, so inefficient that they have to enlist fingers or artificial symbols of various kinds to count even small numbers accurately. In fact they are incredibly large, beautiful and sophisticated *analogue* machines, of whose workings we are only beginning to glimpse an understanding.

Here again, I am delighted to find that Charles Jonscher – this whizz-kid technocrat who ought to know what he is talking about – also thinks that our generation is vastly undervaluing analogy and the power of our minds, and placing far too exclusive a faith in hard, digital logic.

For years I have been following the artificial intelligence (AI) debate, conscious of how central it is to the question of whether, ultimately, people like doctors can be replaced by machines, and whether it will eventually be better for everyone if life is constrained more and more completely by rules. That is why I have been interested in Roger Penrose's insistence that there are aspects of human reasoning which will remain forever beyond computation. And that is why I have watched advocates of so-called 'Hard AI' such as Marvin Minsky who insist on the opposite, as indeed Alan Turing[65] himself did – that all of the functions of the human mind, including self-awareness, feelings, conscience, love, *everything*, can be reproduced by electronic computers when they get big enough and complicated enough, and that that will be soon. Alan Turing went so far as to predict in 1950 that computers would be able to think (i.e. they would pass his own Turing test) within 50 years. That means by now.

He was wrong.

Sir Clive Sinclair was perhaps a more original electronics innovator than Bill Gates, although of course a great deal less successful. He was enormously respected in his day, and rightly so. His Sinclair ZX80, introduced at just under £100 (in 1980, hence the name), introduced a generation, including myself, to computers. But I remember his answer on once being asked what he was most looking forward to in his lifetime. He said, 'Conversing with electronic computers on equal terms'.

He was wrong.

Similarly, Sir John Cockcroft, a hero of my boyhood, who with Ernest Walton at Cambridge's Cavendish Laboratory 'split the atom' and subsequently shared the 1951 Nobel Prize for Physics. He solemnly agreed to shake my hand while visiting our house in Washington when my father was Atomic Energy Attaché at the British embassy. Later, I remember him as director of the Harwell atomic energy research establishment where my father worked, predicting, in what must have been the 1960s, that we would have nuclear fusion[66] within 15 years. After four times 15 years the world has now almost given up hope of controlling nuclear fusion.

So he was wrong as well.

All of these prospects seem more remote now than they ever did before. Jonscher is extremely sceptical about AI and ridicules the press for imagining that mankind was 'humbled' when the supercomputer 'Deep Blue' beat the world champion chess player in 1997. 'So what?' he says. If the room had caught fire, Deep Blue would just have gone on playing. Again, I agree; a steam shovel moves the earth better than a man, but does the man feel 'humbled'?

Four billion years of life and a few million years of the evolution of those primates called hominids have evolved a brain which has a spectacular capacity to learn, feel, drive the body and in various ways reason, but is negligibly adapted to computational or algorithmic logical operations ...

... How we humans have achieved our ability to find meaning in data is as much a mystery as it was in the time of the ancients.

Jonscher gives us a run-down of the state of the art with regard to technology and the Internet, but the emphasis is much more measured and considered than in similar books of a few years ago. First, American hospitals invest more on computer technology for administration than in the wards and operating-theatres. Secondly, budgetary discipline disappears whenever any project includes the word 'computer' in its title. Thirdly, despite all of the money that has been spent, there is no evidence that computers have increased pro-ductivity in industry.

In the end, the book's message is that however marvellous compu-ter technology may be, and it is marvellous indeed, the vastly greater wonder is the human mind.

Jonscher shows how naive it was to think, as people certainly did, that each neurone performs a function analogous to that of a single transistor in a computer. And that all we have to do to make a com-puter we can program to *be* a brain is to make one with a 100 000 million transistors – the number of neurones in the brain.

But what about those 80 000 connections per neurone? Just for a start. And what about the quite different mechanisms we know about, which I had already encountered in *New Scientist* and else-where. For example, there are other kinds of cells in the brain which we tend to forget about, which are far more numerous than even the neurones, and of unknown function. And there are com-plex mechanisms involving sophisticated chemical messengers transported though the labyrinth of fluid channels in the brain. These are just the ones we know about so far.

For Jonscher points to even greater wonders. Within *each neurone* there are 100 000 (or so) protein microtubules, *each one* capable of folding itself into more than one configuration and therefore provid-ing a plausible mechanism for the encoding of information. Here the 'switches' would be only a few atoms across, and at this level Joseph-son and Penrose (again) have suggested that quantum effects may come into play.

So, while the naive view has been that by extrapolating advances in computers we will, by about the year 2010, have constructed a computer to 'match' the human brain, in that it would have 100 000 million components, we now see that even if we were right to ima-gine the brain as a digital device whose power depends simply on the number of switches it contains, even by that crude, mechanistic con-ception of how it works, that complexity may just have increased by 100 000 times.

There is a cultural divide here. Computer engineers talk of matching the power of a brain. Biologists look into their microscopes and wonder if we have matched the computational power of a single one of its cells. We don't just have the computational power of a single computer in our heads; the true comparison would be with a figure more like **twenty billion**[67] *computers.*

Shall we say that all in all there is plenty of scientific evidence that what is going on in our heads is much more mysterious and awe-inspiring than has often been assumed?

The Corrosion of Character, Richard Sennett

I was driving to a home visit in my car one day when I heard a voice on the car radio speaking 24-carat good sense about the way in which the new, hard, impersonal business world is damaging human values. Richard Sennett, an economist at the London School of Economics and in New York was discussing his new book, *The Corrosion of Character.*[68] It is about the personal consequences of work in the new capitalism – the stupidity of society being run for the selfish interests of corporations who make a virtue of their disinterest in the long term, their lack of commitment to individual employees, and their assumption that the employees will have no long-term commitment to them.

> *But I do know a regime which provides human beings with no deep reasons to care about one another cannot long preserve its legitimacy.*

Sennett bases his book on several case examples. Some commentators have criticised or even ridiculed it on these grounds. They felt that valid commentary should be based on analyses of large numbers of examples, itself a fascinating illustration of the cultural divide we are dealing with. Which is reality? The personal, or the overview? (I have an answer, but we'll come to that.)

Sennett's first example is of a woman who ran a chaotic but warmly human New York bar which he sometimes patronised. He tells how she decided to go away and improve herself in a modern job, and how the bar then fell into modern management. She didn't like the improved job she went to, and the customers didn't like the improved bar. So she came back and everyone lived happily ever after.

I thought that this was another book everyone should read. Another straw in the wind of change I am finding so hopeful and refreshing.

Other books

Of course I have read books selectively to support my thesis. If I had wanted to argue that there was no alternative to us submitting from now on to the steely grip of impersonal system, because human qualities are nothing but a liability in the modern world, I am sure I would have found plenty of books to support that line of argument, too.

But I have found plenty of good, authoritative support for my real thesis, which is the opposite – that the human qualities of individual human beings are just as vital in the modern world as they ever were. That they are not only the *why* of life, they are the *how*.

Nor would I presume to make the sort of statement you might expect me to make: 'It all began with . . .' Even after studying the subject as much as I have, I have no idea what the change 'all began with'. I suspect that the new approach gradually emerged. I am sure that it is partly a reaction to the arid scientism, materialism, selfishness and authoritarianism of the 1980s, although there is a lot more to it than that. However, I can point briefly to a few more pieces of writing which seemed to me to be significant developments.

David Greaves' *Mystery in Western Medicine*[69] was one of the first books to signal the approach of a new enlightenment in medicine. It was an exhaustive analysis of 'the paradox that mystery thrives throughout medicine, but within a system which seeks to deny it'. He was one of the first to point to 'false dichotomies', in this case between 'facts and values in medicine'.

I saw this as a development of the thinking that attracted so many of us in books like Pirsig's *Zen and the Art of Motorcycle Maintenance*,[70] Capra's *The Tao of Physics*[71] and Toffler's *The Third Wave*,[72] all books which suggested that mankind needed to make some kind of new synthesis between art and science. All of these books were regarded with suspicion, when they were not completely ignored, on the official level. Yet it is easy to imagine that the same people who were acting as high priests of mechanistic scientism in their official lives were reading these books with enjoyment and even understanding in their private lives. That is another glimpse of the dichotomy.

The idea that it might be scientifically respectable to acknowledge the dichotomy between art and science began to gain ground in medicine quite recently, and the movement began, as is entirely appropriate, in general practice. And although the Royal College of General Practitioners (RCGP) can be accused of having in the past 'sold out' the true nature of general practice to technocrats, there is no question that it is from within the RCGP that the exciting recent stirrings have come.

Many people see Iona Heath's John Fry monograph, *The Mystery of General Practice*,[73] as the turning point. It was perhaps then that views which had seemed subversive, dangerous and not to be taken too seriously, when expressed by James McCormick in *Follies and Fallacies in Medicine*,[74] or by Petr Skrabanek in *The Death of Humane Medicine*,[75] or indeed by myself, crossed a subtle boundary and began to mingle with the mainstream.

When Brendan Sweeney gave the Royal College of General Practitioners 1997 James Mackenzie Lecture on *The Place of the Humanities in the Education of a Doctor*,[76] saying things like, 'The greater the expansion of our conceptual framework, the deeper our understanding of the problems of our patients', his words were acclaimed at the highest levels of the profession. The President of the College, Professor Denis Pereira-Gray, emerged as a powerful advocate of personal medicine. The RCGP occasional paper entitled *The Human Side of Medicine*[77] by Martyn Evans and Kieran Sweeney was another straw in this refreshing wind. Everywhere, increasingly confident voices began saying that strict, scientific procedure and analysis is essential for modern medicine – *of course it is* – but that it is not *sufficient* for modern medicine.

Let nobody doubt that this message, which I fervently trust will soon once again appear to be self-evident, *needed to be stated*. And let no one doubt that it still needs saying today.

In another recent book, *The Rise and Fall of Modern Medicine*,[78] James Le Fanu puts the problem as follows:

The paradox of modern medicine that requires explanation is why its spectacular success over the past 50 years has had such perverse consequences – leaving doctors less fulfilled and the public more neurotic about their health.

In this book I am attempting to explain that paradox.

Some recent papers

The emergence of a more sophisticated official view of general practice, incorporating both its scientific and its artistic aspects, is being mirrored in medicine at large by the emergence of an increasingly well-articulated alternative view. In particular, the dominance of the fundamentalist evidence-based approach is now being convincingly challenged.

Clinicians in general have always had instinctive reservations about their practice becoming regulated and governed by protocols. But this does not mean that administrators, politicians and the media are right to accuse them of being 'dinosaurs', mindlessly opposed to all change.

They have become less worried by such accusations, even when they are sometimes levelled by colleagues. They have seen the speciousness of the argument that change must be embraced simply because it is change, and they have started to ask for justification for that change. They have, in effect, begun to ask (and none too soon) that the whole movement from personal clinical judgement towards what we might caricature as 'medicine by numbers' should *itself* be subjected to careful scrutiny, and not just brought in because its proponents think that its benefits are self-evident.

In other words, it ought not to be *too* much to ask that the introduction of evidence-based medicine should *itself* be based on evidence. It is a crowning irony that the greatest advocates of the scientific rigour of evidence-based medicine are so certain that it will do good that they do not believe the possibility that it will do harm needs to be tested. They are so much in the ascendancy that they can simply ignore suggestions that it should be.

Yet the whole idea of evidence-based medicine came into being as a response to the thalidomide disaster.[79] Thalidomide had been welcomed and promoted by its makers specifically because, unlike the alternative drugs for sickness in early pregnancy available at the time, it was extraordinarily free from side-effects. It is almost impossible for us to remember today, but until the thalidomide disaster the possibility that drugs might have serious hidden side-effects simply did not arise in the public mind. Drugs were seen as wonders, as self-evidently good. People were enormously enthusiastic about taking them – antibiotics for every infection, slimming tablets, and so on. An extraordinarily high proportion of the population took barbiturate sleeping tablets every night. Nothing could possibly go wrong . . .

The *Journal of Evaluation in Clinical Medicine* devoted its entire May 1999 issue[80] to 'Advancing the evidence-based healthcare debate'. It contained papers from all over the world, some of which describe ways of enforcing evidence-based practice more effectively, but most of which raised questions about the evidence, or lack of it, upon which evidence-based medicine itself is based. To venture a simple summary of the gist of this complex and authoritative document, I would say that evidence-based medicine goes wrong when it stops trying to help and when it starts trying to control – in other words, when it stops being a tool and starts to become a master.

Some recent ideas: the postmodern conference

'My personal highlights? Iona Heath's extraordinary and wonderful Pickles Lecture . . .'

'But the last word must be about Iona Heath's pinnacle Pickles Lecture on the last day – wow. I felt humble and exhilarated at the same time.'

'The highlight of the conference was beyond doubt Iona Heath's shining Pickles Lecture. I cannot remember standing in a unanimous ovation to an academic lecture before. Even less can I remember being reduced to tears by one. Iona gave such a masterly display of eclecticism . . .'[81]

It seems a long time ago now since the Royal College of General Practitioners Spring Meeting in Cambridge in April. It even seems a long time since May, when the above reactions to the meeting were printed in the *British Journal of General Practice*. But the feeling of something wonderful stirring remains.

I claim a certain amount of credit for this particular success. Iona had found me in the foyer before the lecture and said she had a job for me. I had to sit near the front of the hall and let her know how long it took me to read her slides. I did this, reading them at a carefully-judged pace and giving her a nod which was efficient, confidence-inspiring and appreciative, without being a wink. Subtly done. The result can be judged from the extraordinary notices she received.

I love College Spring Meetings, and go to them most years. They are each held in a different regional centre. I was on the organising committee for the one we hosted here in Wessex[82] in 1994. The extraordinary response I received to my *Paradox of Progress* session at that meeting gave me the confidence to go ahead and get my book of the same name published.

We had taken the bold step at that 1994 meeting of running four sessions in parallel (previously it had never been more than two). I argued against it in the planning committee on the grounds that it might lessen the feeling that everyone had shared in the same experience, but I was out-voted and it all turned out successfully.

I was wrong.

This year in Cambridge there were up to *seven* sessions running in parallel, and it really was impossible to go to everything that one wanted to. Choosing one particular event on the Friday afternoon, for example, meant missing no less than *12* others. Another example, perhaps, of the increasing problem of getting into the spotlight of attention.

I was explaining these reservations to a fellow delegate in a coffee interval at the meeting, balancing a hot mug, miscellaneous documents, brochures, and plastic goods bearing advertisements for heart drugs, and he said he liked the arrangement – no one told you what to do, you just designed your own conference, did your own thing – it was a *postmodern* conference.

Two weeks later, visiting Dublin for another conference, I would read 'Only dull people are brilliant at breakfast' among the Oscar Wilde epigrams engraved on his memorial in the park across the road from his childhood home. But that was too late. The next morning in Cambridge I broke the ice brilliantly at breakfast by announcing that I didn't know what postmodern meant. I told the person innocently eating his muesli across the table from me that people seemed to use the term 'postmodern' to refer to anything trendy of which they approved. I found I was talking to an expert.[83]

There and then he gave me a succinct introduction to the subject and followed up with emailed references, so now I am an expert, too. And none too soon – years ago the lady who had reviewed my book for the *Health Service Journal* telephoned me to say that she thought I was the first postmodern GP – it sounded the sort of thing I ought to be pleased about, so I said I was. Now at last I know what she meant. The structured, scientific, *don't-worry-your-pretty-little-head-about-this-and-just-take-the-tablets-or-you'll-die* approach to medicine is 'modern'. The unstructured, do your own thing, slop about in trainers, *let's-sit-down-and-talk-awhile-I'm-interested-in-your-anger* approach is 'postmodern'. Paternalism *v* patient autonomy.

Actually, neither of these is really *me*. I'm a muddy compromiser. I prefer a doctor–patient relationship that is founded on mutual respect and trust, but at least I'd traced the source of my long-standing confusion – I had always assumed *modern* meant *contemporary*. Once I realised that *modern* meant, well, *post* – I mean, post what had come before when it *was* contemporary – it all became clear. Modernist is to modern as impressionist is to impression. They are movements in the history of ideas. Modernism, in short, is bad, whereas postmodernism is good.

Some of the time.

One thing I got out of the conference was a strong feeling that there is a tension between these two approaches, that both have their cohorts of utterly convinced activists and both are riding at full pelt for the bright horizons of progress *in opposite directions*. One of the things which made Iona's William Pickles Lecture so riveting was that she tackled this dichotomy head on.

A hard act to follow

She had the hardest of hard acts to follow. At the coffee break we had emerged to cross the sunny Churchill College quadrangle, saying to each other, 'That was quite extraordinary. That was a *wonderful* experience.' But an hour later Iona had made Professor Sir Roy Yorke Calne, at the peak of his brilliant form, seem like a warm-up.

However, a very special warm-up which was perfect for the *Art and Science of Medicine* theme of the meeting. A great man *par excellence*. Icon. Ellis and Calne, *Lecture Notes in General Surgery*, bible for my surgery finals – clear, concise, authoritative, invaluable, and compulsory reading indeed, if you wanted to pass your exams. A pioneer of renal transplant surgery ('When we discovered cyclosporin[84] . . .'). Wow.

But today he was talking about art. *His* art, to be precise (and he was). Gentle, quiet, immensely impressive. First a résumé of classical paintings of medical subjects, then his own paintings, mainly of his own patients, before and after transplant surgery.

'How long do the pictures take?'

'About 12 hours.'

'Do the patients mind?'

'Not so far, no one has ever refused. Sometimes the first thing they say when they come round after their transplants is, "When are you going to paint me?"'

The faces, the bodies – expressive, strangely coloured, getting better, getting worse. The stories – this one happy, this one tragic. An understated, consummate, moving, modest, indescribable performance. I won't try to describe it, except to say that the Royal Academy Monet exhibition a few days later had nothing on it, and I doubt that the Rembrandt self-portraits at the National Gallery two days from now will either, wonderful as they are, of course – but seeing someone fitting his art into such a rich life – amateur art, I love it.

'A masterly display of eclecticism'

Iona takes the stand after the break, wearing her ceremonial college gown lightly, accepting the Pickles medal from the President graciously, and starting to talk about 'dualities' and 'uncertain clarity'. Difficult ideas, expressed with clarity. I start to read her slides silently for her, mouthing the words at a careful pace:

> *An inevitable dualism bisects nature, so that each thing is a half, and suggests another thing to make it whole . . .*
>
> Ralph Waldo Emerson

Down to the bottom, and turn, and nod, 'OK, go on – I understand, I think'. She smiles and carries on.

Her starting point is Michael Frayn's play *Copenhagen*, currently running in the West End, which so brilliantly clarifies Heisenberg's uncertainty principle of quantum mechanics for the layman.[85] The way in which the fundamental constituents that go to make up atoms, and thus the matter of the universe, are particles when we look for particles and waves when we look for waves, and never both at once. (John Gribbin expressed this memorably in his book, *In Search of Schrödinger's Cat*: 'In 1906 JJ Thompson received the Nobel Prize for proving that electrons are particles, in 1937 he saw his son receive the Nobel Prize for proving that electrons are waves; both father and son were correct.'[86])

Iona Heath uses this deeply mysterious duality as an analogy for a series of dualities which are inherent in the mysterious reality which is our personal experience of general practice. She quotes the words which Michael Frayn gives to Neils Bohr, the great man *par excellence* of twentieth-century nuclear physics, in *Copenhagen*, which spell out the extremity of the difference between particles and waves:

> *... particles are things complete in themselves. Waves are disturbances in **something else** ...*
>
> (my emphasis)

'Yes, I think I understand ... like panzer tanks and butterflies ... *completely* different, one or the other, one *and* the other, never both at once ...' Smile and nod. 'Please go on ...'

She continues with the duality between the particular and the general. The individual patient is infinitely varied and interesting – lumped together into a group which shares a common disease, they lose that individual fascination but acquire an entirely different *kind* of fascination. We learn much by generalising from the particular, but it is dangerous because it makes us forget to see the individual. We must do both:

> *Science can tell us nothing about an individual. Science speaks in terms of probabilities, of means and standard deviations, the behaviour of groups of electrons or proteins or people, not of individual entities.*

Everything that makes an individual an individual, everything that importantly defines an individual's life, is outside the realm of science. The practice of medicine involves only individuals.[87]

And her solution, the one which excited me so much? It is that we must learn to use an 'oscillating gaze'. When we look for the individual we must see the individual – when we look for the group we must see the group.

So I want to argue that we should stop torturing ourselves with conflicting dichotomies, but revel in the enhanced understanding they can give us.

Revelling in the enhanced understanding

Here I have given a personal selection of landmarks in the new enlightenment which is dawning at the turn of the twentieth century. There is a new realisation that our minds are vastly more than they seem to be, and that we have been selling our own strengths short, not just quantitatively but also qualitatively. And that reality is not fixed and digital, but that it teems with paradox and duality.

It is also bringing a realisation that we can cope with this, because coping with reality is exactly what our minds are so exquisitely evolved to do. They are not just machines that are ludicrously bad at doing sums – they are something more than machines and they are wonderfully (and deeply mysteriously) adapted to modelling the world, if only we will let them do this. So modernism is dead, and postmodernism rules OK. We have grown up, we know better – let the new millennium begin.

Were it not, that is, for the group of people I mentioned just now who are riding like mad in the opposite direction. Now we must try to accommodate *that* duality, which will be difficult because we have to accommodate it within the primitive, rigid, digital machine which is the over-mind of society. And that common mind, in which we all share, is not good at doing that kind of subtle task. For all its impressive ability to do sums, the over-mind of society is stupid.

How shall I choose the words to mark that face;
Unerringly to pick it from the throng?
Shall I use 'pale' and 'aquiline' and trace
The jaw-line that my finger runs along?
Shall I record the angle of that eye
In cold degrees, and then the length of nose –
So many millimetres? Shall I try
To count the forehead-wrinkles in repose,
And then again when fury knits that brow?
Shall I compute the curling of those lips
To quantify the love it justifies?
But measured thus the fond expression slips,
Uncalculated teardrops fill four eyes.
　　When I can bear to venture love again
　　I'll drop the maths and just set free my brain.

CHAPTER NINE

Grasping the nettle: the tough questions

Doctor Willis, why did you prescribe the first tablets?
6-year-old boy, after the first tablets didn't work

Everyone knows the best way to win an argument – you spot the weaknesses in your opponent's argument and demolish them.

Wrong. What you must do, if you really think you are right, is *ignore* the easy answers, as winning those points will not affect the real case you are attacking at all. What you must do, and we have Karl Popper[88] to thank for this insight, is look for the *strongest possible* case against what you are saying. You look for your opponent's *best* points and answer *them*. What is more, if your opponent has not expressed his points with their fullest possible force, you must do this for him, or again your argument will be in danger of failing. If you can do all of this and still win, you are getting somewhere.

Geraldine's party

I'm at a dinner party for Geraldine's sixtieth birthday. Shouting over the band at Mary, managing director of an international science journal, and John, an American professor of neuropathology. The potential of computers is enormous, they say. GPs could have a model of medical experience on their desks; when they use a drug they could feed in a profile of the features of the patient they are treating and match it to the profile of patents in the trials of the drugs and choose the one that fits them best. Why don't they – why don't *we* – do it?

I tell them about the young *Sunday Times* journalist we met on holiday in Crete at Easter, who wanted us to call him 'Mr Nick', walking with us down the Imbros Gorge, little son in his back-pack, jumping sure-footedly from rock to rock. He has no time to be ill, work would be completely unsympathetic if he was, and when he does go to a doctor he just wants to be fixed – no time for the fuzzy bits.

He's got a point, and it's difficult to answer. So has an editorial published in the *Independent* this week – of course we should have league-tables of hospitals, of doctors, what possible objection could there be? Someone has been listening along the table and shouts over the amplified brass, 'Will the NHS be here in 10 years?' He can see the point of it, but he doesn't want to have to wait for his hernia operation.

Difficult questions . . .

I thought I was getting somewhere, back in March. I had been asked to write a commentary for the *British Journal of General Practice* on the decision of the GMC to run regular re-validation tests for doctors.[89] I was in correspondence with both the President of the RCGP and the Secretary of the British Medical Association (BMA), and both of them had had the draft of my article. Both were sounding intrigued, sympathetic even, with my belief that the whole approach was fundamentally misguided, but they both wanted to know what I was suggesting instead.

The *British Journal of General Practice* had sent my article to Sir Donald Irvine, President of the General Medical Council (the GMC is the third, with the BMA and the RCGP, of the main professional bodies affecting GPs), and asked him for a commentary for them to publish next to it. So there was one weekend when all three of these eminent doctors must have been spending at least some time considering what I was saying and wondering what was wrong with it. I was looking forward to Sir Donald Irvine trying to take apart what I had said. I almost hoped that I was wrong, because then I would be able to relax and get on with my life. After all, I had no doubt that I would be able to comply as easily as the next doctor[90] with what the *Guardian* described enthusiastically as 'the new checks',[91] and I would have a lot more time to sail my boat.

You see, I'm not playing a game here. I'm not a lawyer fighting to exonerate a man he knows to be a crook, a debater trying to win a case he doesn't believe in, a company employee putting his duty to the profit of his firm before the safety of his fellow men, a teacher fulfilling a check-list curriculum instead of transmitting a genuine love of the subject, or a politician lying in order to win an election. No, I am trying to ascertain a truth. Something absolute. Something *beyond*. I am as interested in being wrong as I am in being right. I am not trying to *win anything*. Have we got that straight? I doubt it.

But Sir Donald Irvine didn't have time to write a reply (I was told), and the *British Journal of General Practice* just published somebody else's disappointing repetition of well-worn arguments which did not address any of the points I had made. It was hard to be sure that the author had even seen my piece. The President of the RCGP told a mutual friend in a telephone conversation that I had raised important points which 'needed addressing' – which was briefly encouraging. The Secretary of the BMA stopped writing to me. Busy man, of course.

Everybody seemed to be taking the line of least resistance. Perhaps they had also been at birthday parties where people said they wanted their doctors to be checked up on, infallible and networked together, and they were weary of trying to think what was wrong with the idea. Because one thing is certain, almost everyone knows that there is *something* wrong with the idea.

So what *is* it? That is the subject of this book. Now is the time to grasp the nettle.

Now is the time to construct that super-strong case. 'Come on then, Dr James . . .' says Mr Nick in the Imbros Gorge, resting on the grass below the towering cliffs, his wife getting out their sandwiches, us getting out our bottle of water, their son sound asleep in the back-pack propped up in the shade of a tree, '. . . set out your stall, what are you actually suggesting?'

OK, Mr Nick, here you are, I hope you're listening.

Never mind the easy targets:

- evidence-based medicine has never been subjected to its own criteria of validation
- re-validation of doctors was brought in on a spurious pretext – a PR exercise to show some response to a scandal (the Bristol heart surgery affair) it would have done nothing to prevent[92]
- league-tables for schools distort the curriculum and make schools reluctant to enter borderline candidates for examinations

- information technology has not increased the productivity of industry, and has produced hardly any of the epidemiological breakthroughs which were so eagerly predicted (not least by me)
- recruitment and/or morale are falling in medicine and other front-line occupations
- the raising of standards and reducing risks make people *more* worried about those risks, not less
- the individuals carrying out the regulation process have shown just as much human frailty as those whom they regulate.

All of these points have been made many times, and it hasn't made the slightest difference; the ship sails on. We need to do something much more difficult. We need to go to the questions which worry us *ourselves*, even if they haven't been thought of or expressed clearly by the enthusiasts for regulation – the really tough questions, that is – and answer *them*.

The really tough questions

The really tough question for me is this. Technology has improved the safety and reliability of cars, aeroplanes, cross-channel ferries and drugs. Some of this is the result of market forces, but most of the benefit comes from regulation – the only way to get airlines all over the world to conform to safety standards is to *make* them conform, to inspect them to make sure that they are doing so, and to ground their planes if they are not. When you are flying high above the plains of Africa you are not the least bit sympathetic to the notion that it would be in everybody's long-term interests if aircraft maintenance workers were allowed the stimulus of learning from their own mistakes. Why should medicine, teaching or social work be any different? Is it not absolutely natural and reasonable that patients should be certain that they have doctors who conform to safety standards which are supervised and enforced by as automatic and reliable a system as can possibly be devised?

There is a second tough question. If society were to acknowledge that people in low places often have a wisdom which is denied to those in high places, how does a just society that is seeking to maximise the contribution and the potential of all its members decide which voices it will listen to?

And there is a third question. If I really believe that it is an unrealistic objective and even a selfish indulgence for any individual to try to elbow their way into the unimaginably narrow spotlight-beam of media attention, and that they should look for their satisfaction in the things that lie close around them, what the hell am I doing writing a *book* about it? Am I that most despicable of human life-forms, the hypocrite, who says 'Don't do what I do – do what I say'?

Let's take the first question first.

We are using a wrong model

Society has got its model wrong. People are not clones, like Boeing 747s, all out of the same mould, built to a formula, with everything about them understood. One day the application of a rigid mechanical model to human beings and human life will seem to have been incredibly naive. At the moment we are powerfully entrapped in the illusion that people really *are* like 747s. One day, perhaps it will be soon, we shall realise that we are not only different from Boeing 747s in size, shape and the materials we are made of, but that we are completely different *kinds* of things – Panzer tanks and butterflies, waves and particles, individuals and societies – there are useful lessons to be learned from the comparison, certainly, and some useful tools derived, but these lessons and tools are of limited, not (for heaven's sake) *universal*, applicability. I think the belief that people can be as well maintained as 747s if we apply *exactly* the same approaches will come to be regarded as one of the most idiotic delusions in the whole of human history. It is all the more absurd for being held by a society which trumpets its belief in its unprecedented rationality. In retrospect we are going to look much more like a society which is playing with a new toy. The toy is information technology, and we are learning the hard way that it is far too dangerous to be given to children.

The models aren't good enough

'Come on,' I said to a group of friends the other evening (the group has been meeting every couple of months for many years at one or other of our homes, for informal discussions about matters which interest us), 'I want the strongest possible arguments that doctors should be regulated.' Rod, with a background in computer sales and local government, rises to the challenge:

'I see what you mean, the objections you raise to models are perfectly valid, but surely that just means that we need better models. We all know that school league-tables are unfair at the moment – grotesquely so – a school in a middle-class area will always score higher than a school in an inner-city problem area where the staff are working their socks off in infinitely more difficult conditions, and so on. But although the government is dragging its feet over introducing value-added tables like the ones in the *Guardian*, they will come, and with other improvements like that the tables will get better and better.'

'But that's the fundamental point, isn't it?' I say. 'What we have really done is to move from working on reality to working on models. We are creating a kind of virtual reality. In the past when you wanted to know whether a school was good you went and looked at it, now you look at the model – the league-table – instead. The question that interests me so much is, do we go on trying to improve the models, or do we decide that relying so much on models is fundamentally misguided?'

'But how on earth are parents going to make an informed choice of school if they haven't got hard facts to base them on?'

'But we've just said that "hard facts" can be grotesquely misleading. I suspect that the kind of people who are going to use league-tables would have had a pretty sophisticated understanding of the relative merits of the schools in their area just by using the old techniques of visiting the schools and talking to people in the area.[93] Just think of the huge amount of time, money, energy and motivation being expended on collecting data to construct the models, all of which could then be returned to actual teaching.'

'But how do you choose a doctor without some sort of scale?'

'Ask the neighbours for their recommendation. Best of all, ask a local district nurse or midwife, if you can find one who will really tell you what they think. *They* know what the doctors are like. But don't whatever you do pay attention to league-tables. The kind of doctor who will score highly on all the checks is the kind to avoid at all costs.' I see John and Peter are nodding vigorously in agreement. 'What do they measure, for heaven's sake? All our patients die. In the end. *All* of them. It's quite appalling . . . Something has got to be done about it . . .'

There is general laughter – death rates were just the sort of thing they were thinking you *could* measure.

'Look,' says Rod, a little resentfully, 'you asked for the strongest arguments . . .'

'Yes, I'm sorry. I'm very grateful.'

The politicians have got to do something

Brother Andrew is on the phone tonight. He meets politicians through his chairmanship of the National Association of GP Commissioning Groups, and he knows how they think. 'The politicians have got to do *something* to fulfil their obligation to deliver equal care to everybody.'

'But there will be no end to it', I reply. 'The idea of equal standards is an illusion. However high standards become, by definition all but one of us will always be less good than the best, and half of us are going to be below average. No matter how high the standard becomes and no matter how enormous the effort required to keep it there, it will be the same. We are all doomed to be failures forever.'

I launch into another of my hobby-horses. 'People get confused about the meaning of the word *excellence*. It means to excel – to be an *exception*. It is impossible for everybody to excel. The doomed quest for universal excellence will do – is doing – immense damage. If the politicians believe in universal excellence themselves, they need educating. (You know the one about the Minister who was shocked when he was told that half of all doctors were below average. He wanted something done about it.) And if they *don't* believe it, then they are just being dishonest with the electorate, and that's worse.'

'But what would *you* do,' says Andrew, 'if you had to solve the problem of unequal standards?'

'I would try to get us all to understand that life will always be unequal – that's life. It may be a hard message to get across but we have got to try. There is no other way. We *can't* all have rose-covered cottages half a mile from Charing Cross – which is what estate agents say everybody wants – however nice it would be.

Anna Russell got it exactly right in the parody she did of a Gilbert and Sullivan song, when her simpering heiress Pneumonia Vander-fella sings, "Things would be so di-if-fer-ent, if they were not as they are . . ."[94] It may be tough, but things *are* as they are.

'It may not be quite as easy to see why we shouldn't be trying to create a world in which everyone has a doctor who is above average, or why medicine can't be made more infallible if we treat doctors as robots. And I'm not saying that we shouldn't be treating doctors as robots just because that is an inhuman way of treating our fellow people. That's not the point. I'm saying we shouldn't be doing it because it *doesn't work.*

'It is counter-productive. Doctors who are forced to work as robots will no longer be doctors, and people *need* doctors. There is some kind of doctor equivalent in all cultures, and there always has been. The exercise of independent judgement – within some kind of framework of professional rules and conventions, of course – is an essential ingredient in the formula.

'Karl Popper proved half a century ago that Utopianism, the search for a perfect world with all problems solved, inevitably leads to authoritarianism.[95] We saw Utopianism tried in Communist Europe, and that's exactly what happened. At one time communism as an ideal was extremely attractive to a large number of Western intellectuals, but it *doesn't work.* "From each according to his ability, to each according to his need" sounds absolutely wonderful, and nobody could possibly object to it, except that it doesn't take account of human nature.'

Areas in which society has seen the need to step back from rigid control

I'm lucky to have a brother who will put up with this sort of thing, but I'm not stopping now. 'I have been thinking of examples, prece-dents, this kind of change in public perceptions. I mean, for example, the way in which we have come to accept, by and large, that censor-ship does more harm than good. There are lots of kinds of publica-tions, films and shows that we loathe and detest and would prefer people not to see, but except in extreme cases most of us agree that it is better for our society if we allow the maximum possible freedom for artistic expression. The purpose of censorship in the arts has been successfully shifted from *restricting* what can be seen to *maximising* what can be seen.

'Another example is that most of us in the UK would have much preferred Rolls-Royce to remain British. Just the same with Land Rover and MG. But by and large – reluctantly, but by and large – we have come to accept that it is in the overall economic interests of the country if we allow the kind of market freedom which permits such firms to be taken over by foreign buyers. Because then our own firms can enjoy the reciprocal benefit of acquiring interests in other countries.

Examples of hard lessons that society has generally accepted

- Censorship should be minimised
- Speech (and the press) should be free
- Business freedom should be maximised
- Innovations should be scrutinised
- Doctors should not prescribe 'a pill for every ill'

'So, I am suggesting that as a society we *could* come to understand that it is in our own real interests if we allow a much wider variation of clinical practice than we instinctively think desirable, and much less central control of individual practitioners than we think we want. And while we are at it, we could learn that looking to find a culprit for every mischance in life, and particularly in medicine, and seeking legal redress, compensation, revenge or whatever it may be is only rarely in the interests of society, and often is not even in the interests of the people who get the money. Talking to patients makes me certain that the general public would understand and accept this kind of wisdom a good deal more readily than the politicians and the media think.'

'Well,' says Andrew after we have talked for a long time, 'it's time for bed. I start at six these days. I shall be interested to see what you write.'

So will I, because I am certain of one thing: we do need controls, and we need to make them definite. A silly, extreme example is that we need to know which side of the road to drive on. But how far do we pursue that argument before we get to rules which tell us when to eat our greens, when to cut our hedges, when to send birthday cards, and in the extreme of Orwell's *1984*, when to think a thought?[96]

How do we decide which controls are necessary? That is another really tough question, and although I have no proper qualifications for saying so, I think this is the central dilemma of management in the modern world.

> I only want to know my doctor's sound,
> I really don't think that's too much to ask.
> Of course I wouldn't wear him to the ground,
> Just check for rotten apples in the cask.
> If zero-defect-tolerance applies
> In making cars, then how much more in life?
> A man insists on safety when he flies
> so why not when he contemplates the knife?
> And when you come to choose your children's school
> The key-stage SATS[97] are where you start to look.
> The doubter of league-tables is a fool
> We want our offspring learning by the book.
> And so we sing the new millennial song
> And nothing (much) can possibly go wrong.

CHAPTER TEN

The pathology of managerialism

'I said to my manager last week, "You're making me bad." He said,
   "I make everybody bad."'
'He's probably proud of it.'
   *'Yes, he **was** proud of it.'*

Surrounded by the madness

Christopher, with whom I share the 17-foot day-sailer that Lesley and I towed to Cornwall this Whitsun, has just called by after doing his vasectomy clinic at what remains of our local hospital.

He retired six months ago, and apart from some locum work (including some of mine during this study-leave), his vasectomies are the only medicine he does any more. He is despairing about the managers at the hospital: 'They speak a different language to me. They can't decide anything without having a meeting. I say to them, why can't you just *do* it? They don't understand. It's not their fault, it's the system.'

'Who are "they"?' I ask.

'The nurses. The nurse-*managers.*'

He shrugs, 'I'm glad I'm out of it'. Which I am not – he is a great loss. Then he remembers something – suddenly delighted, he knows I'll like this one: 'Do you know, they've taken the rocking-horse out of the orthopaedic out-patients waiting-room. The children used to love it. They've decided a child might fall off. It's never happened, of course...'

Yes, I like that one.

Some of my best friends are managers

One of my best friends is a manager. I have, as I will tell you, done some managing myself. But on the whole I don't like managing other people and I don't like to *be* managed. Which has always been fine, because the level playing field of NHS general practice was just like that, we were the top and the bottom of the tree, answerable to our individual patients first, to society second, and with no one above us and no one below. The NHS employed us as the patient's agent, no more.[98] In a world which is so wedded to managerialism, I am always surprised that more notice was not taken of how well this arrangement worked. Why was it (nobody seemed to want to know) that nurses needed layer upon layer of managers above them whereas GPs needed none? Were they such very different types of people?

This is what makes NHS general practice such an instructive scenario for a discussion of these issues just now. Nothing short of a management revolution is engulfing medicine and changing everything. WB Yeats' phrase 'All changed, changed utterly'[99] was used by Richard Smith in a much-quoted *BMJ* editorial about this phenomenon.[100] And 'all changed' everything certainly is, but people in low places do not share Smith's enthusiasm for the change, or his conviction that it represents progress.

For some time now it has seemed to me that management is a good idea which has undergone malignant change and become a disease of society. As such it seems to be the most important disease I ought to be trying to treat. In this chapter I shall discuss the pathology of managerialism as a way of recapping the story so far.

But first, two caveats should be mentioned.

- Management is essential to society. To attack the bad points of managerialism is not to deny this – and certainly not to deny that individual managers do superb jobs. Many of them are among the most admirable and important members of our society. It is precisely *because* management is essential that it is vital we do it properly.
- Raising doubts and questions about management is not subversive. Because the ideas of management and authority are so intimately entangled, it is the natural tendency of law-abiding citizens (such as myself, believe it or not) to feel that it is so. But

nothing could be less justified. Healthy management must welcome, if it doesn't already eagerly seek, feedback from those who are being managed. Unhealthy management may not seek such feedback, but that is one of the things that makes it unhealthy.

The nature of authority has changed

I began this book by saying that something has changed radically in society's conception of authority, and that this change has coincided with the microelectronics revolution and the new found ubiquity of information technology.

So here we have an example. The change from subjective (relative) authority to objective (absolute) authority, and the belief that life can be defined by a system of rules, both ideas which are implicit in managerialism, have not come about primarily because they are good ideas, but because they are now, thanks to the information revolution, technically *possible*. At the same time, front-line experience, backed up by Gödel's theorem and other mathematical arguments, strongly suggests that the new tools have hidden limitations – that ultimately they don't work – and that in the end they cannot deliver the certainty they promise.

Making models: structure and reality

I model, therefore I am could be the motto for a school of management. The creation of artificial models of life is the essence of modern management. Managers create models which seem more real and more reliable than reality itself, and which are easier to manipulate – *much* easier to manipulate. Managerialism deals with virtual reality in preference to getting its hands dirty with real life, and it makes a virtue of doing so.

That makes it extremely important to recognise the fundamental but deeply hidden ways in which all models, however sophisticated and refined, differ from the reality they are intended to represent. And to recognise that we cannot avoid the illusion that models appear to be more like reality than they actually are – that we cannot prevent ourselves doing what a child does when it interacts with a doll exactly as if it were a baby. The point is that, while models are useful as tools, they are not as good as any of us – managers and doers alike – imagine them to be.

Our minds, on the other hand, and just as importantly, are far *better* at modelling than we think they are. They have a complexity, subtlety and flexibility which we take for granted because it is natural, but which is exquisitely adapted for faithfully representing reality and coping with life.

Management creates models in order to *plan*, and the resulting plans can only be as good as the models upon which they are based. Fundamental limitations inherent in models of life may therefore explain some of the frustrations we on the front-line are experiencing with the new way of doing things.

For example, until the advent of the new managerialism, we had a simple way of deciding whether we had sufficient district nurses in our geographical area. We just noticed whether they were too busy or too slack and adjusted the numbers up or down accordingly. A ridiculously, laughably, contemptibly simple method. The same method was used to distribute resources right across the health service. It sounds incredibly sloppy these days, but the forgotten truth is that it worked well and was extremely efficient. Most of the time the health service just got on with the job of serving health. What we did, in effect, was to pay attention to the edges (*see* p. 68), the interesting bit, and let the great bulk of the operation look after itself just as long as it ran without problems.

Come the revolution this was not enough – *everything* had to be modelled, everything measured, timed, recorded and compared to norms. Applied to one aspect at a time this looked (perhaps) like sense. Applied right across the whole of the of the NHS, the largest employer in the UK, with every service having for the first time to be individually costed and charged for, it added up to an operation of vast complexity and enormous extravagance. We shall never know the cost of this counting of the cost, because the experiment was never controlled. But one thing is certain, the passionate voices protesting at the time that the concept was fundamentally mistaken were utterly disregarded.

Managerialism was brought to the NHS in the late 1980s and early 1990s by people who believed in it, and in the fact that it was 'progress', with a faith of truly religious intensity. That some of us did not get burned at the stake for questioning it is no more than an accident of history.

The same revolution has occurred over the same period of time in all of the other public services (except the law, for reasons which remain mysterious but which may have something to do with the fact that so many Members of Parliament are lawyers). *Everything* now has to be measured and modelled. Things that were simple human interactions have now been elaborated into numerical transactions. Everywhere, organisations are requiring their employees to send bills to one another every time they give each other advice on the telephone, and to spend the hours of their days constructing time-charts to show how they spend the hours of their days.

Again I am not exaggerating or joking. Over and over again the whole thing is regarded as completely mad by the people who are being forced to apply it, but over and over again the people doing the forcing regard it as the epitome of progress.

Mat, my future son-in-law, works as an Environmental Health Officer and knows all about time-charts. *Everybody* I talk to today, except Lesley and myself, knows about time-charts. Even I, Lesley points out, complete sheets (which get more complicated every year) for out-of-hours visiting. But Mat has to spend at least half an hour a day doing his time-chart.

'At *least* half an hour . . . So you mean more like *three* hours a week than two and a half?'

'Yes.'

'And inspectors all over the country are doing the same thing?'

'Yes. Everybody does it. In everything.'

'And it is all public money?'

'Yes.'

And it is all *completely ridiculous*. He is only allowed half an hour in his time plan to do it. The first week in the new job he got the procedure wrong (this was hardly surprising, because he was coding all of his activities from an index consisting of three closely typed A4 sheets), so it took him three hours to do the whole thing again. But he was only allowed to say he had spent half an hour on the time-sheet, so he had to make something up for the rest of the time.

He is fairly meticulous, but by and large he says people do make up what they put down. He may, for example, be visiting a new area and walk down a street making a list of the business premises. Putting down a particular business and a particular activity for each ten-minute time-slot in the chart is obviously impossible, so you just fill up the slots with something that looks plausible.

Everybody knows that this happens, and how useless the information is. No one even looks at it when it has been filed – in that, therefore, at least some degree of economic responsibility is still displayed. All of the important things are duplicated anyway – any sensitive case which might involve litigation is documented separately, and everybody knows that the two records, which ought of course to be identical, never match up.

The conclusion is unavoidable – that the whole business is a ludicrous game, nothing but empty process at huge public expense. Being seen to 'do' the model is more important than doing the *thing*. It is completely mad. Do you see why I am so desperate about this unbelievable, monstrous imbecility being foisted on the health service I love so much?

'Apart from anything else, it's incredibly insulting to you. Not to trust you.'

'Yes', says Mat, to whom I unhesitatingly entrust my daughter, 'it is *very* insulting . . .'

Modern life is even fuller up than we think it is

Modern life seems to be full, but we can't begin to comprehend *how* full it is. Everything is even more complex and even more difficult than it appears.

Again and again when we look for things on lists we find that the thing we want seems to be the only thing that isn't there. And this happens however long you make the list. The UK has spent tens of millions of pounds of public money on a system of READ codes intended to give doctors a reliable, specific code for every disease and procedure in medicine. Even after decades of development it is full of anomalies and gaps, which are a source of amusement[101] to those who use it in surgery, as I do, but which have rendered the system so far almost completely useless (as pointed out by the Audit

Commission) for reliably representing medical activities and making meaningful comparisons between times and places.

And the same applies to plans. Time and again the contingency that confronts us in reality turns out to be the one that has been left out of the plan. This doesn't mean that fate has got it in for us. What it means is that reality is many orders of magnitude more complicated than we think it is – as simple as that, as complicated as that.

We go on making the mistake of underestimating the complexity of reality because our brains cope with complexity so automatically, if we let them get on with it. Contrary to all contemporary assumptions, it is the *machines* that have problems coping with reality, and management goes wrong when it does not let the human mind get on with the job. It is instructive to use the *find-and-replace* function of a word-processor to substitute the word 'interference' for 'management' throughout official documents. And this, incidentally, is an example of the kind of thing which a computer does much *better* than the human mind.

Management goes wrong when it insists on everything being recorded, when so often this is simply for the benefit of management in the construction and maintenance of its proxy models. Time and time again when I ask patients what has changed to make their lives so much more stressful, they say 'paperwork'. Again, the thing that is special about paperwork is that it is immutable. You can't push it aside and squeeze it up to allow room for other things – it is one of the fixed things in life, it takes up its space, and that is that.

'At least half an hour every day filling in the time sheet . . .'

'Why don't you all just say, "No", Mat?'

'It's a disciplinary matter. It's in your contract. You have to do it. If you don't somebody takes you aside and has a word with you.'

Somebody, presumably, who hasn't got the guts to say how lunatic the whole thing is . . .

Give me strength . . . And when the managers imposing the paperwork are actually using *false* models which fail to reflect the full complexity of the lives they are presuming to manage, as everything in this book confirms they inevitably do, that is where management goes wrong. That is where you get the problems. (Do I have to go on spelling this out? Yes I do, yes I do.)

There is another distortion in the paperwork picture. Everyone thinks that *their* bit of paperwork is the exception to the rule that 'paperwork is excessive'. Just as patients seem to think that it is everyone *else* who comes to you with problems that are 'trivial'. Like the government's *Patients not Paper* initiative, which has done nothing to stem the rate of increase in the volume of paperwork in the health service, but which was announced with a massive brochure which crashed through the letterbox of every doctor in the country.

I would announce my measure to limit paperwork on a single address label. It would say '"Excessive paperwork" is the thing *you* are asking me to do.' Or, more properly, for Mat, or for the vast numbers of other people who are less fortunate at the moment than doctors, '. . . is the thing *you* are *telling* me to do.'

The absolute, change, the new and entrapment

The propensity of our individual consciousness to become entrapped by absolutes, by change and by the new is not merely mirrored but *amplified* in the technical world.

Management goes wrong when it becomes entrapped by absolutes and certainties. Nothing is certain in life except death. Every death in medicine may seem to be a failure. But if the individual has difficulty avoiding the dominance of hard figures and absolutes over soft feelings and judgements, still more does the managerial mind. Just as we cannot prevent our judgement about someone being overruled by their rank, by their score or by the class of their university degree, to an even greater extent human judgements in management are crowded out by measurements and labels, however crass and invalid these are known to be.

Everywhere we see managers using measurements and targets as proxy markers for reality. I have always regarded it as a failure if I do not get a woman with a suspicious breast lump seen at the very next out-patient clinic. A moment spent imagining the agony of a woman in that position tells you that a wait of any time at all is failure. But now we have a much-trumpeted national decree that cancer patients 'must be seen by a specialist within two weeks', and provided that that target is achieved, management is able to chalk up an absolute, 100% success. Another analogue-to-digital conversion, and one that produces an absolute nonsense.

We have evolved with the capacity to see only movement, change and the new, and to leave the unchanging whole out of sight in our subconscious. The managerial world goes wrong when it carries this natural tendency to the extreme, so that it is obsessed by change, lives for it and lives *by* it. A positive feedback loop in which change feeds on change comes into play, like the explosion in the size of peacocks' tails which must have occurred as soon as peahens got the message that size matters and began to exercise their preference for the largest on offer. Nobody gets famous for their services to stability. Everyone wants to make their mark on the world, and that means changing things. So before long we all get trapped in a whirligig of accelerating change. Does this sound familiar?

When you examine what people who urge us to welcome change, and who run courses in the management of change, are actually saying, you nearly always find that they are promoting *their* change. They want us to move quickly to do what they want. But people working on the front-line of life find some of their greatest satisfaction in managing their *own* change. It is often forgotten that one of the adverse side-effects of centrally directed change is that it is profoundly *inhibitory* to *personally directed* change, and therefore profoundly damaging to this cardinal human motivation.

No society in history has survived long on a policy of changing everything at increasingly frequent intervals. In 1996 I had the privilege of playing Tevye in a local production of *Fiddler on the Roof*, and I had to deliver the last line of the great opening number, 'Tradition', which explained it like this: 'Without our traditions our lives would be as shaky as – as a *fiddler on the roof*!'

Thou shalt be busy

I have a memory of a television news item about the rise of the new managerialism in the NHS in 1990. It epitomised the evangelical zeal with which this new kind of medical elite set about their task of 'reforming' the Health Service – changing its ethos from that of a *service* to that of a *business*. The broadcast came from a meeting of health service managers in Southampton, and showed them excitedly practising the new buzz-words of American management-speak on one another. The picture fixed in my mind is of a young woman bobbing into shot with a manic gleam in her eyes and saying, 'We're all workaholics here.' Exactly, I thought, like Kermit the Frog in the *Muppet Show*.

It made me want to say 'But what are you *doing* about your addiction?'

One of the pernicious effects of the new managerialism, which follows from its narrow, obsessive focus on the 'bottom line', is the busyness culture. 'Thou Shalt Be Busy' might as well be the eleventh commandment.

Or rather 'Thou Shalt Be *Seen* To Be Busy'. The pressure is on all over the working world. Given Alton's railway line to Waterloo a proportion of its population, and therefore of my patients, commute to London. They leave at 6.00 a.m. and return home at 8.30 p.m. or later. I hesitate to quote these figures for fear of starting a rush to break the record. They tell of offices where there is a stigma attached to being the first to leave in the evening, and you have to find ways of filling the time until some strong-minded soul makes a break for it and everyone else can grab their coats and bolt for the tube.

There is another positive feedback here and it has got out of control. It applies as much to holidays. Even Sundays are no longer sacrosanct. Once designated a compulsory 'day of rest,' partly in order to stop unscrupulous industrial-revolution mill-owners working their employees every day of their lives until they died, its abandonment today has left information-revolution employees vulnerable to what is essentially the same exploitation.

Doctors have always been prone to the 'busier-than-thou' syndrome, but curiously, and perhaps as a direct result of this (because they feel less need to *prove* their busyness), many of them now organise their lives so that they have a considerable amount of secure leisure. And they work incomparably better as a result.

People do not thank doctors for being tired. During my six months off, circumstances have compelled me to return to work in my practice for one morning, one evening and two nights. That small amount of work, with me fresh, smiling and unfathomably cheerful, has been followed by two letters of appreciation (one of them declaring that I had saved the writer's life, which I hadn't) and someone else telling me in the street how nice I had been to their friend. This may be chance, but I don't think it is. I could normally go for six months with less overt appreciation (except, of course, at Christmas). There is no question that we all do our work better for having a rest, and firms who work their employees to the point of illness – whose victims we see more and more frequently in our surgeries – are being not only irresponsible but stupid.

I often tell people about the many occasions when I have arrived home after work on a music-rehearsal evening feeling exhausted and drained, sometimes wondering whether I am actually ill. But because I am committed to a production, I pull myself together and make myself go to the rehearsal, and over and over again I come back two hours later feeling fresh and vigorous. Some activities in life seem to use up energy – I think of them as 'exothermic' activities – and others *give* you energy – 'endothermic' activities. It is a commonplace that everything is done by people who are busy; perhaps this is one of the explanations.

If managers are looking for something legitimate to change, this is it. Consider the possibility (and forgive me if you regard this as self-evident already) that driving employees too hard might make them do their jobs *less* well. I am a poor linguist and have only halting management-speak, but the term 'counter-productive' seems to be appropriate in this context. The 'bottom line' (another term I know), even from the narrow interests of the company itself, lies somewhere *beyond* merely making employees busy. The real interests of the firm, and beyond that the real interests of us all as a society, lie in trying to contribute to a world which is worth living in and in which it will be possible to *go on* living.

So encourage your employees to go home at a sensible time, to feel good about having proper holidays, to recover from their illnesses, to get involved in plenty of recreational activities, to spend time with their families, and to support local activities. These are the benefits that our generation was supposed to be enjoying, thanks to our era of unprecedented technological achievement. No change would be of so much benefit to employers and society. And if you don't believe this, then why not at least offer to pair up with a similar firm that *does* believe it and do a controlled experiment? They do it, you don't – and watch the difference grow. Or prove me wrong, of course.

Old-fashioned tyranny

One of the worst consequences of the new way of managing things through mechanical systems instead of through human judgement is that it has disrupted the well-tried methods of selecting people for advancement to senior positions. The types of people who get promoted today tend to be the ones who know how to play the game of promotion and who know how to use the systems and get their ticks in the right boxes. It is a matter of common experience that they are often people who are less interested in the human aspects of life.

This is not an evidence-based statement, but it is part of the common experience which I am setting out to represent. What is more, it is no more than we should expect if we replace human judgement with mechanical selection procedures that are designed to deliver objectivity and accountability. We need to consider the possibility, again regarded by many ordinary people as self-evident, that this change may do more harm than good. However, the danger of mechanical systems is that their deficiencies are never anybody's fault, because they are systems. And nobody has the job of pointing out that the systems have themselves escaped the accountability in the name of which they were originally set up. Again the theme recurs, like evidence-based medicine itself not being evidence-based, mechanised selection processes, introduced to ensure accountability, are not in principle accountable to anybody.

However rational we consider the world to be, it is permeated by human impulses such as lust for power, status and control. Newspapers are full of the stories. Ever since the infamous 'Me, Me' generation of the 1980s, it has become respectable to be open about these proclivities, and even proud of them. While many people are in positions of power for altruistic reasons (although altruism itself is increasingly regarded as suspect), it is inevitable that some of them are there primarily because they like the power, the money and the celebrity status. Abuse of power is perhaps the oldest of human failings,[102] made all the more loathsome when it assumes a mantle of self-righteousness. Many of my patients would agree that managerialism at its worst has become a modern tyranny.

Managerialism becomes most overtly tyrannical when it moves beyond the personal and becomes an inhuman system from which no one can escape – automatic, unyielding and inflexible. We all agree that those time sheets are mad, but no mere human has the power to stop the machine grinding on. *1984* was a warning. Surely George Orwell hoped to prevent anything remotely similar from actually occurring. Now that so much of it *has* occurred, the meek way in which it has been accepted is genuinely alarming.

The thing that is so frightening about Ionesco's theatre-of-the-absurd allegory, *Rhinoceros*,[103] is that while the population of the village is turning one by one into rhinoceroses and stampeding across the stage in clouds of dust – the Nazi take-over, of course – the only reaction from the dwindling human population is to discuss politely whether they are 'black' rhinoceroses (with one horn) or 'white' ones (with two).

A civilisation which does not protect its citizens from tyranny can hardly claim to be advanced.

The new enlightenment:
post-management

For more than 20 years I have been the 'GP in charge' of our health centre treatment room. The four practices of doctors jointly employ six nurses to work in the centre, and they provide all the normal practice nursing services and also a minor accident service to the town, because it is 15 miles from the nearest casualty department.

A few years ago, as 'manager' of this team, I came under pressure to fall in with modern management ideas and to do 'appraisals' for the nurses. In the end I agreed to do it, but only on the understanding that the doctors and the patients already knew that the nurses were doing an exemplary job, which was the simple truth. The interviews were to be directed solely towards helping them and listening to what they had to say. I thought briefly of calling the interviews 'praisals', but settled for 'biennial review' because it sounded less twee and made it clear that I wasn't going to get involved in the process every year.

I certainly didn't want to use the term 'appraisal', because I knew it was none of my business to 'appraise' an independent professional colleague in a sister profession, and to adopt the term would be to buy into an implied hierarchical structure running completely counter to the working relationship of mutual respect which had been the key to our success for so long.

So that's what we did. The message was 'you are all doing a good job, we want to "praise" you. Come and share your feelings as colleagues. This is your opportunity to take a personal interest. It is all about mutual respect. Genuine wish to help.' Wishy-washy stuff.

It worked.

I learned several lessons from this exercise. One was that it was a big effort. It takes quite a long time to fit relaxed personal interviews with six nurses and two receptionists into a working life which is already more-or-less full. Another was that it was rewarding for all concerned. Yet another was that the benefit lasted and you didn't have to do it often. I mean *really* not often.

The next lesson was that records (the only bit that outsiders with whom I have discussed our experience have ever wanted to know about) are the least important aspect. I started with a check-list and rarely filled it in. Soon I had the structure in my head and abandoned the check-list altogether. The important thing was to write down positive points that needed action, and then actually to do something about them. I could see how easily filling in a check-list and filing it away could become an end in itself. What is more, just as with patients in surgery, you need to be sure that *they* are sure that when they say something is 'confidential' that means, quite simply, that you won't pass it on to anyone else.

Of course it was hopelessly improper management, and hopelessly politically incorrect. In the modern world it is anathema for doctors to 'manage' nurses anyway. No structure. No records. Not the sort of thing you learn on a management course. But it worked – simple as that. It worked because I was free to do it in my own way and to use my common sense. How can I prove that it worked? I can't. But everyone thought it did, and kept asking me to do it again. Which, after about four years, I eventually did.

I am aware that some people will draw the opposite conclusion from the fact that the nurses liked the personal interviews. They will think that this means they were unsuccessful. This is what I mean when I say we are dealing with two completely different approaches to life. The *bottom line* of my approach was that our treatment room continued to work outstandingly well, the patients regarded it as one of the best features of the town in which we live, and the same nurses stayed for years and enjoyed their jobs. That was what I was trying to do. It was not my objective to 'do management'. I had a proper job to do as well.

To do the model or to do the thing – that is the question. Are we playing a game or doing the thing? I was doing the thing. By that criterion I was reasonably successful. More successful, I think, than some of the people who play managerialism and go home satisfied with a hard day's work well done, leaving the medical profession to patch up their victims' wounds.

Perhaps I am the first post-managerialist doctor-manager, deliberately returning to traditional values and including managerial techniques when they are appropriate, but not as ends in themselves. Steering strongly to avoid the whirlpools of empty, self-serving process. Yes, it would be nice to think that.

My wife is a very good biology teacher (she wants me to say 'very experienced', but really she is very good). For the last 12 years she has worked in a private school, which means that they have been largely spared the phenomenal growth in external interference which has afflicted state-school teachers during that time, causing so many of the best staff to leave. ('You don't mind so much the first time they change everything . . .' said an old singing friend, retired early from a career as a wonderfully gifted teacher, in the car on our way to a charity concert a few weeks ago '. . . but then six months later they decide they were wrong and they change it all again. And then six months after that they change it all *again* . . . and you think to yourself, "*What am I doing this for?*"')

I have watched over the years and know that Lesley has an extremely good record of being right about the stupidities in each wave of changes, and I remember many occasions when practical problems she pointed out straight away at briefing meetings were quietly changed a few years later, without the slightest acknowledgement or apology for the enormous trouble they had caused in the meantime. But above all, the thing that annoys is the way the next wave of changes are brought in with *exactly the same* arrogant certainty that they are inevitable and right.

Lesley's headteacher has decided that they will have an inspection next year, and one of the senior managers (they started having senior managers at the school this year, no *junior* managers so far. . .) has told her to prepare a lesson plan for every lesson for the whole of next year to show the inspector. She says she won't, and will be happy to explain why not to the inspector. The senior manager (also a long-standing colleague) said he would love to be a fly on the wall.

So would I. She is quite willing to prepare lesson plans for the week of the inspection itself to show the inspector what she is doing, but after 25 years of apparently effective teaching, she would like to know what the problem is that they are trying to solve.

She already has a detailed scheme of work for each class that she teaches. For the lesson with the first-years on locusts, for example, she just writes 'locusts' in her planning diary. Do they have a problem with that?

Describing a face in a photograph makes you *half as good* at recognising it afterwards (*see* p. 95) – *that's it*. I'm not a bit surprised. And I wouldn't be a bit surprised if writing a simplistic list of aims and objectives for every one of the lessons that a teacher has been refining for years would make her *teaching* half as good. We are not talking here about an occasional exercise the teacher has to do – we are talking about a new, pointless, regulatory chore which has to be done for every lesson, for ever, before she does any of the actual teaching. Which quenches the spontaneity which is so often the spark which lights up a lesson. *That* is why it could so easily make the teaching half as good, and *that* is why it sounds like madness. It is happening absolutely everywhere at this moment.

Anyway, I support her. If those of us who are near to retirement and financially secure don't speak out for sanity, the inspectors will soon be demanding a barrow-load of documents for every lesson for every pupil. Then two barrow-loads. That is hardly an exaggeration, and certainly not a joke. The reality is beyond parody – and certainly beyond a joke.

The tough questions

Managerialism seems to go wrong the more it becomes separated from the thing it is managing. The separation of managing from doing is not new. What is new is the erection of an artificial model between the two, and using the model as a way to manage by remote control. When the model takes over and starts to serve itself, things start to go *very* wrong, particularly when we fall for the illusion that the model possesses human abilities such as understanding. One of the tough questions that managerialism ought to be asking itself is why this innovation has never been tested. If the benefits are held to be obvious, why have they never been demonstrated?

For example, the enormous cost of computerisation has never been formally justified. Perhaps because there are too many vested interests, and the whole thing is too much fun, to risk finding out the truth.

In fact, any of these new ideas may have serious unwanted effects. They are at far too early a stage to be regarded as being out of the experimental phase. If they were new drugs they would certainly not have been given their product licences.

There are many ways in which assessment and interference with the independence of professional men and women may do harm – for example by removing personal motivation and responsibility, diversity, flair and richness. In the field of medicine I believe it will remove an essential element of what it means to be a doctor. In state education I fear it has already removed an essential element of what it means to be a teacher.

Doctors all over the world believe sincerely and with passion that professional freedom is essential to their role. Among them are good, intelligent people. Not all of them are speaking from selfish motives. There exists the possibility both that they are right and that this revolution in the way the world seeks to motivate professional people may do harm – perhaps *enormous* harm. There exists a possibility that so much empty process and such a mindless collection of meaningless paper *are already* doing enormous harm. There exists the possibility that managerialism needs to be substantially changed. Managerialism is a faith that has never been tested. Since accountability and rationality are among its central tenets, it should not be too much to ask that it should apply these principles to itself.

There is a cartoon strip in *Dogbert's Top Secret Management Guide* in which a manager is demonstrating to his team a dog that has been trained to sniff out waste in an organisation. In the second frame the dog has its nose pressed hard against the manager and is pointing an arrow-sign straight at him. In the third frame the manager is saying, 'We'll begin as soon as he's done playing around'.

I am afraid that the problem with too many managers is that they have immunised themselves against this kind of feedback. They have stopped being 'us' and they have become 'them'. *They* have broken the feedback loop. *They* have forgotten to listen quietly.

Listening quietly is what doctors ought to be good at. That is what I tried to do with the treatment-room nurses. Mutual respect is the key. The person who knows the job best is the one who is actually doing it. I didn't bother with structure or records in the end.

I wasn't doing it 'properly'. There exists the possibility that that is why it *worked*.

This morning I told Lesley that I had woken at three o'clock thinking the whole idea of this sabbatical and of writing this book was pointless. I was Canute trying to stop the tide coming in. Everyone I spoke to was being drowned by it. Everyone was filling in time sheets. Doing a bit of tidying up last night I had found the briefings about this awful thing 'clinical governance' awaiting my return to work next week.

'I should move on to the next chapter on Utopia this morning,' she said as she got out of bed, 'that'll cheer you up.'

'I'm afraid the point is going to be that Utopia is an illusion.'

'Oh dear, you don't want to end up depressing everybody.'

'I know . . . that's the trouble . . .' Then I remember Julia Cameron's book, *The Artist's Way*,[104] which was so helpful by the bedside light in the early hours and got me happily back to sleep. 'But if I constantly think of the audience I won't do anything worthwhile. I've got to say what I think, and in the end I know what I am trying to say is positive . . .'

Lesley brings me my breakfast in bed (just this once), and after a few minutes I am in Utopia.

We've modified a worker not to sleep,
We've done it in a smart, genetic way.
Our clients say we've made a quantum leap;
They keep the blighters working night and day.
We've had a few objections from the church;
Trade unions made a fuss. That was before
We got them banned from harming our research
And drove a coach and horses through the law.
So now the way is clear for our next plan;
We've got a prototype that doesn't *eat*.
We're going to sell them packaged in a can
And get our Nobel Prizes for the feat.
But still behind it all the questions lurk,
A man that doesn't eat – just might not work.

CHAPTER ELEVEN

Confronting the Utopian illusion

How can this happen?
Patient at the reception desk pointing out an error
in a prescription

> *Polly Toynbee*: Ian, let me ask you a question: If two babies are born with cerebral palsy in next-door cots, one of them can pin it on a nurse or a doctor, the other can't. They've got identical needs. One baby will get millions of pounds which will be taken away directly from a health service to help care for all of the other children who **can't** blame it on someone – where is the justice in one child getting the money because they find someone to blame and the other not?
> *Peter White*: Ian? . . .
> *Polly Toynbee*: . . . what matters is their **needs**.
> *Ian Walker*: . . . and the answer, Polly, is for the medical service to **stop injuring people**, then you **wouldn't have the problem**.
> *Peter White*: Polly Toynbee, Ian Walker, thank you very much. Thanks for all of your calls. There'll be another chance to 'Call You and Yours' next Thursday.[105]

Breast cancer missed for six months

A few weeks ago there was an item in the local newspaper about a family who had raised a large sum of money in memory of their sister who had died of breast cancer 'after it had been missed for six months'.

Lesley was interested in this because *her* sister died of breast cancer, and the diagnosis was also missed for more than six months. Her sister was living in the USA at the time, so at least it wasn't the National Health Service or the UK medical profession who got the blame. Not that we had really thought to blame anybody in those days.

Anyway, the large sum of money that the local family have raised is going to be spent producing an educational package 'to answer GPs' questions about important cancers' and, by implication, to make them less likely to make these terrible mistakes.

It occurred to me to say something to Lesley that I have never said before, even to myself. 'Do you know, I have *never* missed a breast cancer?'

I mentioned two patients who were also dear friends as examples of breast cancers I *didn't* miss. In each case I knew what it was as soon as they showed it to me, they had seen the specialist at the next clinic and their treatment had gone ahead straight way. Not that it appeared to make the slightest difference, but few memories could have been worse to live with than if I *had* felt I had been responsible for any delay.

But that is the point. Even if you go on like that for your whole career, nothing *shows*. No newspaper headlines say 'Doctor Willis did not miss a breast cancer again today', 'and again today', 'and again today', for 26 years. Instead we wait until one patient, of one doctor, somewhere, *anywhere*, has a delayed diagnosis, and then the implication to everyone who reads the article is that Doctor Willis should be made to use the new educational package and get his questions answered about important cancers, as only a CD-ROM (or perhaps, as the article breathlessly hinted, the Internet) can answer them.

Of course I could miss a breast cancer on the first day I go back to work. I have to live with that constant self-doubt or be a dangerous doctor. Or I could miss one of the large number of different cancers of other parts of the body. I can think of at least one occasion when my diagnosis of such a case was indeed delayed, but even then there were reasons, and it wasn't actually one of the many other occasions in my career when I felt I had really made a mistake, however much and however understandably the family thought (and perhaps continue to think) that it was. Every doctor knows the truth of the saying that the most grateful patients are the ones on whom you make the *worst* mistakes. They appreciate all the attention you give them. They sense the depth of your concern. Patients don't always, or even often, expect you to cure them, but they do expect attention and concern.

The point is that you can never relax. You have to doubt yourself all the time (however many CD-ROMs you have interacted with) – it goes with the job. And if you practise long enough you are going to make every mistake in the book. Statistically, a GP is going to have one of his patients die in childbirth about once in 400 years, for example. And I don't mean by that that it will necessarily be his fault – that would be a lot rarer again, but he has to share the responsibility for making sure it never happens at all, which theoretically *ought* to be possible. So there is a 1 in 146 000 chance[106] – hugely greater than the chance of winning the jackpot on the National Lottery – that it will happen *today* on every single day of my life as a GP. Just as you should ask the driver to stop the car and let you out if you hear him boasting that he is a safe driver, so you should run briskly from any doctor who thinks he is infallible. But the awkward thing is that at the same time you get most benefit from a doctor who feels, and inspires, confidence.

Of all diseases, breast cancer is probably the one to which doctors are most alert. There is something about it. A woman you have known for years, perhaps watched bring up a family, comes in saying that she has a lump in her breast, and you are immediately galvanised. Believe me, you are not going to try harder to get it right because some administrator or some cocky journalist has told you to. If someone comes up with a better way of reliably distinguishing harmless breast lumps from malignant ones we shall all be talking about it the same day (*see* pp. 69–70). It will probably be on the national news. We won't be waiting however many years it takes to produce the next update of the CD-ROM.

But if you go on using the media to stereotype doctors as 'failures' in areas in which they actually have a personal record of total success, you are not only undermining the essential trust of their patients, but you are also jeopardising the self-motivation which is the best, and certainly the best-tested, means of maintaining that level of safety. Both of these things – the undermining of trust and the jeopardising of self-motivation – will certainly do harm, lives may be lost, indeed *will* be lost, as a result, and who will be to blame then? Who will need the education then?

Is that a silly question?

When doing the best you can is never good enough

There is no issue upon which reasonable people are more impossibly divided than the need for the regulation of personal behaviour to make life 'safer'.

My daughter, Becky, picked the heading 'Our intolerance of risk' out of one of my early outlines and said that she thought it was a defining characteristic of our age. The illusion of perfectibility is strong. But standards are getting more and more difficult to sustain as we climb further and further up the slope of progress.

We are judged today not against personal goals, but against *over-mind* goals. It is not enough to adopt standards which will prevent a particular event happening in our personal experience. It is not good enough to adopt standards which will stop it happening in our town, or even in our city. The new reality is that we will be at fault if we adopt standards which allow the event to happen *at all*. The significance of this change has still to sink into the world at large, although it constantly oppresses every conscientious doctor. The effect on human motivation when *doing the best you can is never good enough* is incalculable.

The effect on human motivation if we were to succeed in creating a world in which *nothing ever went wrong* is also incalculable. If nothing ever went wrong, there would be no need to be careful. The child brought up on an empty country road notoriously does not know the danger of traffic. When a generation has grown up never knowing poliomyelitis, because its parents flocked desperately to have them immunised (each of the parents having had personal knowledge of people paralysed or killed by the disease), how will a free society continue to motivate the new generation to get *their* children immunised with the media singing and dancing about one side-effect of one immunisation and remaining utterly silent about a million successes?

The fact is that the futile attempt to live to a standard which will eliminate media-scale risks is destroying the joy of living for individual people in the real world. Probably risks which are only perceptible on the media scale can only be prevented by media-scale supervision, and that leaves little role for the individual. But the truth is that often the minuscule good done by the elimination of a remote, theoretical risk is outweighed many times by the harm done to the independence and motivation of the individual person.

The replacement of individual freedom of action is interrupting the natural cycle of human motivation – it is ultimately futile unless all human actions are really going to be controlled by machines. This is a much more sinister scenario than Orwell's *1984* because it would be welcomed as progress.

Inability to perceive scale

The transcript at the head of this chapter of an unguarded moment from a discussion about the rights and wrongs of medical litigation shows the extent of the entrapment of our society in the Utopian illusion.

Polly Toynbee's question could hardly have been more clearly put. The reply from the trained, logical mind of the lawyer betrayed an assumption that every single medical problem *ought* to be preventable, and that on every single occasion when medicine fails to prevent such a problem it must be somebody's fault. Secondly, it is clear that this trained logician assumed that the listeners to *Call You and Yours* would share his assumption.

The first assumption must be interpreted in the light of the vested interest the legal profession has in a vigorous litigation industry. The second is more significant because it more clearly reflects what the lawyer believed to be true. Society really has fallen for the Utopian illusion, hook, line and sinker, and is applying it to medicine with a vengeance. And once again medicine is only the example – the same applies throughout contemporary society.

My angle on these difficult and frequently debated issues is to show that the underlying illusions are the same ones which we have been discussing in other contexts. Just as inhuman managerialism is a scourge of contemporary life, so is amoral, game-playing litigation, distorting priorities to a grotesque degree and sucking the life-blood of our society like some repulsive parasite. If society truly believes that life ought to be perfect, then nothing and nobody is safe, the protective measures will go on getting more and more baroque in their elaboration, peacocks' tails will seem dowdy in comparison, and life will simply come to a halt.

You can't take a school party near a coast any more unless you are carrying a flotation device of a particular specification. So – guess what – school parties don't get taken near coasts. No lawyer would take them, that's for certain – they wouldn't be so stupid. Lawyers are canny about protecting themselves. A patient of mine who is a solicitor says that *all* the partners in her London firm conceal important aspects of their medical histories from their doctors because they know that if they once get them written down they will never be able to prevent their subsequent disclosure to other lawyers.[107]

From the perspective of society as a whole people will occasionally be struck by asteroids – and somebody, somewhere knows that when this happens the proportion-blind and common-sense-lacking over-mind will be likely to pin the blame on *them*.[108] So 'to protect themselves' they make it a rule that everyone has to go around wearing anti-asteroid hats, or forfeit their insurance – something like that. The rule is absolute: 'No asteroid hat, no insurance. Sorry sir, that's the rule.' It is impossible to fault the logic. And the madness ratchet of the world moves on another click.

Is this an exaggeration? A patient came to me with a bunionette (a bunionette is a painful swelling at the base of the little toe, just as a bunion is a painful swelling at the base of the *big* toe), and I said that the problem appeared to be being caused by pressure from tight shoes. 'Oh yes,' she said, 'I know it is, it's caused by the safety shoes we wear at work in the school kitchen. We *all* have problems with them.'

'Well, do you think you could stop wearing them for a bit?'

'Oh no, we can't do that, we wouldn't be covered by the insurance. We've all got sore feet from the shoes, but we have to wear them.'

Another ratchet click.

Another letter:

'Dear supervisor. Mrs Clover's feet are being damaged by her safety shoes. Do you think you could sort this out with your insurance company. It might help if you suggest that if the safety shoes continue to damage her feet it could be *their* liability...'

The mind simply boggles that any understanding of the world can be so profoundly distorted as to entertain such extremes of absurdity, let alone to assume that they must be imposed on intelligent people and that they represent an authority which cannot be challenged. Indeed, something peculiar is going on ...

The distorted view

We listen to the radio and we hear a presenter conducting a post-mortem analysis of a sensational tragedy. We keep asking ourselves the question: 'How can these people, who do not have to take personal responsibility in difficult front-line situations themselves, be so arrogant, so hectoring, so certain, in talking to those who do? What leads them to ignore the obvious distortions, for they must have worked them out, they are professionals, they know the power of the media, they know exactly how many people are out there listening. They know how unfair and manipulating they are being in highlighting an exceptional case and talking about it as though it is commonplace and therefore of high priority. The sums are not difficult to do. Are they really being as cynical and irresponsible as they seem? Are they really just using these desperate human dilemmas as fodder for a 'story'? Just playing a game? Because if that is the case, to use the words they are so fond of using themselves, 'Something has got to be done'.[109]

The answer to these questions is surprising. It is that these commentators and media pundits are indeed sincere, and that a great many lawyers are sincere as well. But from their exalted viewpoints the illusions and distortions we are talking about apply with exaggerated force. Their view is *more* distorted, not less, and they are *less* aware of it, not more.

I believe that if I moved away from the front-line, if I lost touch with my first-hand experience of daily problems in daily life, I would start to make the same mistakes. Again we have a reality which is the opposite of what intuition leads us to expect. It is natural to assume that the highly professional, technically enhanced, sophisticated view of the obviously intelligent, highly selected, celebrity-status television commentator is more refined, better informed, more reliable and generally *superior* to the simple, brute experience of us simple folk in the street. Or superior to the view of the ordinary patients in the surgery. But in fact, in important respects, it is the *other way round* – the illusions and distortions are bad enough for us down here, nose-to-nose with reality, but they are *far worse* up there.

The words we use reinforce the misconception – 'overview', 'high viewpoint', 'superior'. The image here is of someone climbing a mountain or ascending in a balloon and looking down and seeing the whole view and getting the bit they know about into excellent proportion, but this is a fallacy. When we stand on a mountain and look down on a view, the part of our mind that Guy Claxton calls the *under-mind* (*see* p. 96) surveys and models the *whole thing*. Mental functions of a sophistication we can barely glimpse, which have evolved over millions of years[110] precisely in order to make sense of this view from our unaided senses, select with wonderful precision the flash of movement, the tiny detail that has changed since the day before, the wisp of smoke. The incongruous is picked out almost unerringly from the mass of 'dull' congruity.

But this feat can only be achieved while the mass of 'dull' congruity is modelled in the under-mind, almost entirely inaccessible to the conscious mind. We take it for granted that we are doing the same thing when we view the world through the instruments of the 'media', but we are profoundly mistaken. It is as if we had forgotten to explain about gravity to a correspondent from a different kind of world, so missing out one of the fundamental premises on which they must base any hope of understanding what it is we are describing. So we assume that we have a superior view of the world which is enormously enhanced by the power of the media, but we are oblivious to the fact that the great mass of 'dull' congruity is hardly represented in it at all. We are like Nelson applying his telescope to his blind eye,[111] except that we don't know that the eye is blind.

We watch our television screens and we think that we are seeing the world. We fit what we see into the models that our brain provides, and the models are inappropriate. What we see on our television screens looms larger in our models than events going on in the street outside, in the high street, or in the local hospital. When the television screen shows us a doctor making a mistake, our model says that we are looking at a doctor across the room and *he* is making the mistake. Our confidence in doctors close to us is shaken.

It is easy for us to be persuaded that action must be taken to put right this glaring fault in that doctor 'across the room'. But the only way that that can be achieved is for the action to be made to apply to *all* doctors. And this is the proposal we haven't thought right through. We *cannot* think it through, as we simply do not have the mental equipment to relate the horror story we have just heard properly to the 100 000 other doctors whom our 'solution' will affect. All 100 000 doctors will be subjected to the new rule designed to put right the fault we are so worried about in one of them. Yet some of these, perhaps even the majority, will already be working to personal standards *far above* the ones specified by the new rule. Call me bolshie if you like, but I find something powerfully demotivating in being *told* to do far less than I was doing already. So while the adverse consequences of the new rule ought to be weighed up in this larger context, from the artificially mediated perspective that larger context is completely invisible.

I believe that this is the kind of reason why so many things which seem to make good sense on the media scale seem like madness on the personal scale. For example, we think that we are doing good by restricting people to buying paracetamol in blister-packs of 14 tablets at a time, because we are on a committee trying to solve the problem of self-poisoning and so we see things with the perspective of that committee. We do not see it as our concern that ordinary people think the resulting inconvenience and enormously inflated expenditure[112] are insulting, patronising, and the action of a nanny state gone mad. From our remote vantage point we do not hear the voices of sharp old ladies who want to know whether we intend to ban shoelaces next, then kitchen knives, then first-floor windows. Nor are we concerned that we have undermined the value of paracetamol as a first-choice, safe home remedy, in favour of vastly more expensive and toxic prescription analgesics. Nor are we concerned that a patient taking the recommended dose of paracetamol for the control of long-term pain will have to buy a new pack every second day. Nor that we have just given the world another continuing source of rubbish to dispose of. For we are acting as experts, as specialists. We have focused our lofty gaze and such extraneous matters are the concerns of others.

The end of progress

Our intolerance of risk is linked to our belief that the end of uncertainty is in sight. There has been a series of books in recent years proclaiming the end of science,[113] the end of history,[114] and so forth. Such books begin by saying how often in the past men have believed that they were close to knowing everything there was to know, and how obviously silly it was of them to think so, but that this time it is *true*.

This reminds me of men who come to mend the drains and who invariably say that the ones who failed to do the job properly last time were 'cowboys'.

The central assumption, which underlies a thousand statements by politicians, calls by single-interest pressure groups, and assertions by media pundits, is that the modern world solves its problems, and eliminates risks, by creating rules. 'What are you going to do to make certain this tragedy *can never happen again*, Minister?' One longs to hear a Minister having the courage and wisdom to say just once that they won't do *anything* until they have considered whether the proposed solution will do more harm than good.

On the car radio a spokesman for the Multiple Sclerosis Society is saying that a common resentment among his members is the memory that their diagnosis was delayed. The real problem, he says, sounding certain that the listening world will share his modern approach and that only dinosaur GPs will question it, is 'the lack of national guidelines which all GPs are made to follow'. The number of cases of MS seen by a GP is small, he explains, so how can they be expected to know the warning signs? They need to be *told* the significance of visual symptoms and that they must refer patients immediately to a neurologist. Another problem (he adds in passing) which is *disgracefully* overdue for action is the appalling waiting time to see neurologists . . .

'Rubbish,' I say to myself, drawing into the car park to buy a bottle of champagne to take to my wonderful ex-Gaiety-girl patient's hundredth birthday party, and to get the chemist to make up a medicine-bottle label which says, 'The Champagne. One champagne glass to be taken at frequent intervals until drunk. Alternatively – go on, bathe in it.'

Rubbish. GPs are probably as good as anybody at the notoriously difficult business of spotting early MS. Send every fizzy arm or fuzzy eye to a neurologist at the stage you first see them and the neurologists would be floundering and even more swamped than they are now, as they would be the first to admit. The problem is that the majority of patients who have a single episode of visual disturbance due to retrobulbar neuritis never have any more trouble. (Funnily enough, I know this even though I am a humble GP who goes for years, thank goodness, between seeing new cases of MS. Perhaps I know it because the *possibility* of MS goes through my mind every few days.)

Whether it is really right to burden all of them with the knowledge that they may have the beginnings of MS, while there is no treatment which will make any difference, is an extremely delicately balanced human dilemma. On the whole we are tending to be more frank at an earlier stage than we were in the past, but things could easily swing back so that we are regarded by our successors as heartless dinosaurs for so self-righteously dumping the worry on to our patients. It is not at all impossible that we will be sued for it. I can hear it now: 'And the answer, Polly, is for the medical services to *stop causing patients mental distress*'.

Certainly that is how an older generation would regard our present open attitude, as a cop-out from our professional responsibility, and trends like this tend to swing back, and certainly cannot just continue. If an effective therapy for MS appears, of course, everything will be different, and the case for the earliest possible diagnosis and frank discussion will not need to be made. The thing you can say for certain at the moment is that anyone who thinks they know the answer for certain is *wrong*. MS, with its characteristic protean, insidious, episodic onset is one of the diseases every medical student at some stage decides that he or she has got. And those medical students who really do get it, like an extremely courageous cousin of mine, understand the dilemma as well as anybody.

Giving doctors orders

Mother, leaving surgery with her son, John: 'Say goodbye, John . . .'
Me: 'Goodbye, John.'

Table I: The 'giving-doctors-orders' industry

Date	Name	Description
1858	General Medical Council (GMC)	The long-established self-regulating body of the medical profession, investigates and punishes unprofessional behaviour. Effectiveness increasingly questioned

(continued)

Table I: (*continued*)

Date	Name	Description
1976	JCPTGP (Joint Committee on Postgraduate Training in General Practice)	GPs undertaking training of young doctors, and to a lesser extent training of medical students, are subject to assessment, training and accreditation, with detailed stipulations about practice facilities, etc.
1997	Clinical Governance	New name for local structures of guidelines, protocols and audits. Hailed from on high as a revolution; on low it remains an enigma[115]
1998	PCGs/PCTs (Primary Care Groups/ Primary Care Trusts)	Committees representing geographical clusters of GPs, responsible for budgets and increasingly dictating prescribing and therapeutic priorities
1999	NICE (National Institute of Clinical Excellence)	Establishes national policies for clinical practice, especially prescribing of drugs
1999	The Beacon Programme	'Beacon Practices' provide exemplars of government-recognised excellence
1999	CHI (Commission for Health Improvement)	The enforcement arm of NICE – the *nice police* have already warned doctors who depart from NICE guidelines to explain their reasons for doing so in advance in the patients' notes
1999	Caldicott Guardians	An individual in every health service organisation, for example, in each GP practice, responsible for maintaining the confidentiality of patients' personal information. The author was a member of the Caldicott Committee
2000	NSFs (National Service Frameworks)	Codes of national standards for key conditions and services
2002	Professional revalidation	The General Medical Council's mandatory five-yearly revalidation process for all doctors, likely to begin in 2002

Name	Description
Other agencies (dates not relevant)	
FHSA (Local Health Authority)	Employing Authority – employs pharmaceutical advisers who periodically visit GPs and advise them on rational and economical prescribing
Consumers Association	Ever-vigilant independent watchdog, publishers of the excellent *Drug and Therapeutics Bulletin*
National Health Service Executive	Issues instructions to doctors on an increasingly wide range of issues, especially relating to immunisation against infectious diseases and other aspects of public health
Central government	Ministers are increasingly likely to act as though doctors' primary responsibility is to them, rather than to individual patients
General practice partnerships	Practices commonly have wide-ranging protocols and policies for the management of specific conditions and situations, by which individual partners are to a greater or lesser extent bound
Out-of-hours co-operatives	Out-of-hours GP co-operatives require standards and procedures of participating doctors, especially in the area of documentation
Ethical committees	Clinical research is now subject to regulation and systematisation of sometimes baroque complexity
PACT (Prescribing Analysis and Cost)	An elaborate (and invaluable) national system for collating and reporting to doctors statistics about their prescribing

(*continued*)

Table 1: (*continued*)

Name	Description
Medical defence organisations	Provide doctors with insurance against claims for negligence and support when they are defamed. Increasingly seek to influence doctors towards defensive patterns of practice
The lay press	Pundits give news, advice, comment and judgement on a huge range of medical issues. Accuracy and balance are often secondary to sensation and controversy
The legal profession	Increasingly likely to demand access to patients' medical records, including records of matters which have no bearing on the case in question
The Audit Commission	In early 2000, newspaper reports appeared of the Audit Commission advising patients to ensure that their doctors adhered to standards
Community Health Councils	Statutory local bodies representing the voice of the public in the health service, with wide rights of access to official information

New regulatory agencies and mechanisms announced in the *NHS Plan* of 2000

PALS (Patient Advocacy and Liaison Service)	'Will be established in every trust, by 2002, beginning with every major hospital'
Annual appraisal and mandatory participation in clinical audit	'By April 2001 all doctors working in primary care, whether principals, non-principals or locums, will be required to be on the list of a health authority and be subject to clinical governance arrangements. These will include annual appraisal and mandatory participation in clinical audit'

Name	Description
National Clinical Assessment Authority	'An arm's-length Special Health Authority. Where concern has arisen locally, it will provide a rapid and objective expert assessment of an individual doctor's performance, recommending to the health authority or employing trust educational or other approaches as appropriate'
Independent Reconfiguration Panel	'Citizens and patient representatives will make up one-third of the new Independent Reconfiguration Panel on contested major service changes'
Citizens Council	'A new Citizens Council will be established to advise the National Institute of Clinical Excellence on its clinical assessments. It will complement the work of the NICE Partners Council which provides a forum for the health service and industry to comment on the work of NICE'
Modernisation Agency	'To help local clinicians and managers to redesign local services around the needs and convenience of patients'
National Patients' Action Team	
Primary Care Development Team	
PAF (Performance Assessment Framework)	'Covering the six key areas of NHS performance: health improvement; fair access to services; effective and appropriate delivery of healthcare; outcomes from healthcare; efficient use of resources; high-quality experience for patients and carers. Each year tables are published showing how each health

(continued)

Table I: (*continued*)

	Name	Description
	PAF (*continued*)	authority has performed against the measures in each category ... New efficiency targets will be set'
	NHS Leadership Centre	
	Consultant's job plans	'All consultants will have job plans specified by the employer linked to annual appraisal of their work'
And ...	UK Council of Health Regulators	'Its role could evolve'
		I bet it could ...

There is now a whole industry devoted to giving doctors orders. In the past there was a huge industry devoted to giving doctors *advice*. This is a fundamental change – part and parcel of the change from education to training. Although the line is invisible and we can cross it without feeling a thing, we are in completely new and uncharted territory. But let no one doubt that there is a widespread assumption across the executive level of modern society, shared by the media, and presented to the public as established fact, that medicine is a technical discipline which can be made more and more infallible by a system of ever-improving rules, and that resistance to this idea is nothing more than stubbornness, born of professional conservatism and self-interest.

Responsible behaviour

It is always difficult to question efforts towards perfection. Raising questions about the wisdom of efforts towards greater *safety* is particularly difficult. It is easy to paint such resistance as irresponsible, reckless and complacent. But if looking at these issues with a broad perspective reveals that some short-term moves towards perfection in safety standards are based on illusions, and are already doing more harm than good, then that attempt must be made. Then it is *not* to question the current trends which becomes reckless, irresponsible and complacent.

Some doctors take the view that the government has a huge parliamentary majority, it pays us, and we have got to take our medicine and do as we are told. These are the fatalists. Some of us believe that to take this view is to duck our responsibility.

Another view which some doctors take is that they realise things are going wrong, but that the practical solution is to go along with it and bend the rules to accommodate reality. These are the pragmatists. This attitude is more understandable, but it does not satisfy those who think that the contradictions and the misconceptions have to be confronted, and that appeasement is not the way forward, or things will just go on getting madder until we do have to make a stand, and then it will be that much more difficult.

Isaiah Berlin expressed it thus:

> *The notion of the perfect whole, the ultimate solution, in which all good things coexist, seems to me to be not merely unattainable – that is a truism – but conceptually incoherent . . . we are doomed to choose, and every choice may entail an inseparable loss. Happy are they who live under a discipline that they accept without question . . . or those who have arrived at clear and unshakeable convictions about what to do and what to be that brook no possible doubt . . . those who rest on such comfortable beds of dogma are victims of forms of self-induced myopia, blinkers that may make for contentment, but not for understanding of what it is to be human.*[116]

The perfectly accurate clock

Lesley's watch is running slow this morning, battery running down probably, and she needs it for an examination she is invigilating at school. I offer her my watch for the day. No problem to me – I am surrounded by clocks and I don't need any of them while I'm doing this. I eat when I'm hungry. Better idea – she'll take the neat, high-tech, perfectly accurate bedroom clock from our bedroom dressing-table.

It's a wonderful thing, our perfectly accurate clock. Locked in through radio signals to an atomic master-clock at the National

Physical Laboratory, keeping time to an accuracy of fractions of a second in hundreds of years, and adjusting automatically in and out of summer time.

Except that there is a problem – our perfectly accurate clock is three minutes slow. It may be *exactly* three minutes slow (to thousandths of a second in millions of years), but it doesn't even seem to be that. It was right when we set it up, but it seems to have been getting slowly slower ever since. I am resigned to the fact that you won't believe this. I can hardly believe it myself. Certainly I have a feeling it must be our fault.

Usually the slowness doesn't matter because the *im*perfectly accurate clock in the radio keeps time very well. But it would be better for Lesley's examination invigilation this morning if the perfectly accurate clock was *right*. So I pick it up and experiment with the adjusting knob on the back. No good – the only thing that moves is the alarm time. I look again, but there are no other knobs to be seen. What I am supposed to do is open the case, take out the batteries, go through the set-up routine, reinstall the batteries and then wait for an hour or so while it synchronises with the radio signal. After, that is, I have found the instructions for the set-up routine. Which is why we haven't bothered to do it yet, and instead we just add three minutes to the time it shows in our heads.

Even so, as we look at it together, turn it over, change our glasses, rattle it, it seems incredible that there is really no way of simply adjusting the hands so that they are right. And then we both see the answer at precisely the same moment (perhaps in precisely the same millionth of a second) and we say it together: 'Perfectly accurate clocks don't need adjusting.' Of course they don't. Silly question.

Nothing can possibly go wrong . . .

Lockjaw in the war

One of my older patients was a medical orderly during the London Blitz. I was giving him a tetanus booster when he mentioned that he used to see a lot of cases of tetanus, or 'lockjaw', in the war.

'Really?' I said, 'How interesting. How many?'

'I don't know exactly how many. Twenty after any raid. You know, bomb injuries.'

I knew. Basic bacteriology – bomb injuries would be contaminated by soil, and soil carries the tetanus bacillus. No immunisations. No modern treatment. No possibility in wartime of six weeks paralysed with curare on an artificial respirator to let the toxin wear off – how could there have been?

'What happened to them, then?'

Silly question.

'Died – in the end – all of them. Sounds callous, but that was it.'

One of the great doomed quests of history

You'd think we're nearly *at* Utopia, compared to that. But are we nearly satisfied?

All of the evidence is to the contrary. The better things get and the more remote the risks of life become, the less satisfied, the more worried, the more selfish, the more vengeful and the less understanding people seem to become. Sounds callous, but that's it. Rather turns you off doctoring. Knowing that the nearer to perfection we manage to get, the greater will be the apparent threat of the remaining dangers.

The question, then, is this. Do we continue to pursue perfection and collude with the simplistic view that it is attainable, exploiting technology to its fullest extent and driving ourselves and our fellow men and women into more and more extreme contortions in order to click the next notch of the ratchet? Or do we confront the illusion, however awkward that may be and however apparently humbling, and find a better goal on which to set our ambitions, which is more realistic and more achievable?

The answer is clear. We can no longer duck awkward reality. Technology has given us a thrilling period of accelerated growth towards perfection, but that growth is running into the sands as the unseen, unwanted side-effects build up. Everywhere we see evidence that the cost of maintaining our most sophisticated systems is becoming unsupportable.[117] Our search for perfection and the final elimination of risk from life is one of the great doomed quests of history – as futile as the search for the Holy Grail, the Philosopher's Stone, or scientific proof of the existence of God, each of which, let us not forget, occupied the greatest minds of their day, minds no different biologically from our own.

The reality is that a perfect solution for the problems of life will always elude us. Our desire for perfection will never be satisfied. The nearer we manage to get, the greater will be the apparent threat of the dangers that remain. The collateral damage and the cost of trying to make further progress towards perfection will become unsupportable.

Life is not a simultaneous equation. It does not have one solution. It is solvable in an infinite number of different ways, but not in more than one of them at any one time.[118] Certainty doesn't exist. Uncertainty rules, OK. Postmodernism and post-managerialism are in. Welcome to the real world. *Now* can the millennium begin?

I dreamed about a gleaming, peasant land
Where rainfall dampened night but never day.
Where people built their castles in the sand
Immune from tides and storms and there made hay
And fertile compost out of cares and woes
That weigh today. I saw the happy folk
Who gaily sang and hoed their perfect rows
Of eco-friendly crops. But then the joke
Was turned on me; they mocked my starry aim
To take away all problems from mankind
And build Utopia, in all but name,
in England's far-from-holy daily grind.
    'We are illusion', echoed, 'Trust us not;
    It takes a spotless car to show a spot.'

CHAPTER TWELVE

Understanding

'Do you do pelvic-floor exercises?'
  'Oh no, if I get on the floor I can't get up.'

'Do you speak Welsh?'
  'No, I have a sleeping tablet.'

The Turing test

When you telephone a helpline with a problem installing a new computer program (which, if you are anything like me, is rather often), you experience a real-life acting out of the Turing test. Alan Turing proposed his test as a way of telling whether a machine can reasonably be said to 'think'.[119] He suggested sending questions by some mechanical means to a hidden computer programmed to answer exactly as if it was a human being. By the same method you send similar questions to a real human being and both reply by the same, mechanical means. If you are unable to tell the difference, i.e. which is which, or which is who (or who is who, I suppose), the computer has passed the test.

In the same way, when you call up a computer helpline it is almost impossible to tell whether the person you are talking to, who always seems to be called Hank, is advising you out of his own understanding and experience, or is just reading standard answers off a screen. In fact there is an eerie feeling that it won't take much more progress in the direction of speech recognition and speech synthesis before you won't know whether you are talking to a person at all.

I have a microbiological helpline available from my surgery desk. It is answered by someone who is always called Paul. This is because he is always the same person, at least he has been for the last

20 years. He is also certainly not a computer, because we occasionally meet at retirement parties. In fact he is a consultant microbiologist, and when I ring him, about twice a year I suppose, he invariably tells me exactly what I want to know, and immediately. 'I've got a two-year-old who has just eaten some cat litter ...' 'Oh yes, *Toxocara catis* – people worry because it's related to *Toxocara canis*,[120] but it isn't really a problem ...'

I know you are supposed to get that sort of thing out of a book, or from the look-up function on the practice computer, or else to consult a protocol, or a CD-ROM, or (if you have a great deal of time) the Internet, but I still have the privilege of making the comparison and I can tell the difference for sure. As soon as I look at a guideline my actual worries frequently tunnel through to a combination of circumstances which is far more unusual and specific than the algorithm allows for. A dignified committee has laboured mightily to produce what is in practice an elaborate codified statement of the obvious, which leaves the mysteries I am concerned with untouched. The trained, expert, human mind tells me the exact thing I want to know, or even the thing I didn't know I want to know, and does it, to all intents and purposes, instantaneously.

I am also aware that I may not have the privilege of this kind of immediate access to the trained human mind for much longer. The modern approach is for this type of reliance on human understanding to be superseded. Superseded in the sense that we now have ways of doing things which are superior, more reliable, more efficient and, above all, cheaper.

My object in this chapter is to point out that this belief in the superiority of such mechanical systems is based on illusion. And I am going to have to do better than merely to assert my belief that I can recognise understanding when I see it ...

Working to rule

In my second six-month house-job after qualification as a doctor I had a registrar who called me 'Jimbo' – which I could have forgiven, but it wasn't his only fault. One night he woke me up to say that a child was coming in (we were the surgical team on emergency 'take') with diarrhoea and vomiting. He told me to do a string of tests and ring him when I'd got the results. I was probably tired, but I saw red. 'Well, I'll look at him first, shall I, when he gets here, and see what needs to be done ...?'

'Do it because I tell you', came the order.

A few moments later the telephone rang again to say that no houseman had ever put the phone down on him before, and that I would be reported to the consultant in the morning. I wasn't, as far as I ever discovered, and the incident was never mentioned again. I can't remember whether the tests I did were the ones he had asked for, and I don't think the child was particularly ill. I can't even remember whether I rang him with them at all – I rather think that I didn't – but the incident sticks in the mind as an ugly aberration during two event-packed, exhilarating and tiring years as a junior hospital doctor. Nobody else in that entire time, during which I worked with some truly great people, ever failed to treat me as a doctor.

It happens all the time today.

And I still react in rather the same way. For at least the registrar who called me 'Jimbo' didn't tell me I had to do his list of tests because it was *the rule*. That idea was going to remain unthought for another 20 years.

However, it is certainly not unthought today. It has fallen like a nuclear weapon into the hands of the second-rate, and they know how to use it ruthlessly.

The maintenance man

I am leaning over the nurses' desk in our GP ward at the community hospital, some time last summer. I am writing in some notes, or doing one of the other things that visiting GPs do at nurses' desks, when I begin to notice a conversation that the ward sister is having with a maintenance man.

They are talking about a broken fixing on a patient's bed. 'I know exactly what the problem is,' the maintenance man says. 'It's simple, I know how to do it, I've got the tools. But I'm not allowed to do it. Because I'm not qualified.'

I look up and say something on impulse. 'Why don't you show me and I'll do it?'

He thinks I'm joking,

'I mean, really. Come on, show me. Where is it?' I get up and start towards the four-bedded ward he has been indicating.

He's completely taken aback. He's a nice chap. We get on fine and I don't want to be offensive to him. But I needn't have worried, because his face suddenly brightens. He straightens up and smiles at me with a grin that shows he knows exactly what to say. Like the cat who has got the latest and most outrageously-priced brand of whitening toothpaste. He *knows* the answer and he delivers it: 'But what would happen if something went wrong? You wouldn't be *covered*.'

The magic words. Repeated perhaps a million times a day in the modern world. The *coup de grâce*: 'You wouldn't be covered.'

'Nothing at all,' I reply. '*Nothing* would happen. I'm a free agent. I take my own responsibility for my own actions. I'm a GP. There are very few people like us left.'

Actually, I don't really repair the bed, I get on with doing other things of a more immediately doctoral nature. But I could have done, and I have done such things many times in the past. I suppose in a way I am anxious not to rub in the humiliation to this well-meaning and capable man, who would be so much more fulfilled in a wiser world.

Right to be worried about EBM

We are right to be worried about evidence-based medicine (EBM). The precedents are not good. It would be impossible to invent credible stories of excess which would equal, let alone surpass, the abuses of rules which we experience in our daily lives.

EBM goes wrong when it becomes a rigid, inflexible model. Anyone who pretends that this is not a real danger is simply putting their head in the sand and denying daily experience.

Nor am I referring so much to the perversion of rules which results in so many people being made to jump through ridiculous hoops – the case against that is self-evident. The danger is much more subtle and apparently benign than that. The plain fact is that rule-following is extremely attractive.

Doing things without thinking is easy – children have to be taught that it is a temptation, a cop-out, not the best way. That it makes us vulnerable.

Rule-following is absolute. It is blind, and it produces a terrible, empty certainty. Actions based on rule-following may be *indistinguishable* from actions based on understanding. Identical in every detail, that is. They would pass the Turing test. But in fact they come from entirely different places.

Just as two politicians may well advocate exactly the same policy whilst aiming to move in opposite directions. We now live in a world in which it is increasingly being assumed that the application of formulae trumps the application of understanding. This places us in extreme danger, but we are so mesmerised by the cleverness of our formulae that the broader truth about their consequences is almost entirely hidden from our view.

We are caught in another trap. It is all so wonderfully simple. Politicians, journalists and lawyers have rushed to the heaven-sent revelation as parched desert-travellers to an oasis. All you have to do in order to do medicine is to *follow the instructions*. Paint in the numbers, join up the dots, look up the rule, surf the net, print out the answer. Lovely hard copy, incontrovertible, proof. Everyone can be a doctor now, it's so *simple*. Even better than that, everyone can be the *judge* of a doctor.

Teachers have been in this position for years. Everyone, as George Orwell pointed out, knows how to teach, because everyone has been to school. But now the medical profession, about whose authority the public has always been even more ambivalent, are in this position, too, along with the police, social workers, rail-safety engineers, the list is endless. All changed, changed utterly indeed, by technology.

Joined-up thinking

In some ways Neanderthals were more successful than modern humans. We know, of course, that they were much stronger than us, but it comes as a surprise to learn that they had larger brains as well. There is evidence that the social groupings in which they lived were at least as large as those of early humans. That means that the social interrelationships – crucially important for survival – that they had to track were at least as complex as those of our ancestors.

But the remarkable thing about the Neanderthals, at once their great strength and their great weakness, was that they didn't *change.* They went on for an almost incredible 200 000 years exploiting the harsh environment on the edge of the advancing and retreating northern ice sheet. For almost a quarter of a million years they used the same flint-napping technique – the most sophisticated method known, the Levallois, which is only occasionally reproducible by the most dedicated of modern enthusiasts – to make the heads of their characteristic short, stabbing spears.

The search for the secret of what changed to produce the fantastic technical creativity of modern humans is the central theme of Steven Mithen's fascinating book, *The Prehistory of the Mind*. His conclusion, which he reaches from an archaeological perspective, is that the revolution occurred when the separate 'domains' of intelligence in the brain began to 'talk' to one another. For example, already sophisticated patterns of functioning in the 'social' domain, previously isolated, became accessible to the domain which controlled the use of tools. This *joined-up thinking,* which Mithen calls cognitive fluidity, is what he thinks marked out the modern mind.

But if a modern human were somehow to meet an extinct Neanderthal and communicate with them, it occurs to me that there might be no external evidence whatsoever to reveal this profound difference in functioning. The Neanderthal, with his enormous brain, might well pass the Turing test.

Similarly, if you or I were treated by a 'doctor' who unerringly followed a system of detailed and sophisticated rules, we might have no way of knowing that he didn't *understand* what he was doing. And you might well ask the question, 'Does that matter?' If Neanderthals survived for all that time, you might be forgiven for thinking that cognitive fluidity isn't *that* important.

But that would be to forget the extremely volatile world in which we now live – far more changeable than the edge of the arctic ice sheet. We live in a time of unprecedented change, and we simply cannot afford not to attempt to model it, to remain alert for change and incongruity, to anticipate danger ahead and to adapt accordingly.

The combined 'over-mind', which our society shares, with its specialist 'domains', each priding itself on its exclusivity and its separateness, is perhaps rather like the Neanderthal mind.

The manager of a local nursing home for elderly people recently told me about the ever increasing complexity and stringency of the legislation with which she has to comply. She gestured towards a mountain of documents and told me how people were amazed when they saw it. There were ever higher specifications for rooms, equipment, numbers and qualifications of staff. And now, on top of all this, there was 'a whole lot of new stuff just coming through'. All making the running costs of her home higher and higher.

Meanwhile, another domain of the Neanderthal official mind is working away in the opposite direction. Applying ever greater restrictions to the funding available to support residents in these homes, largely because the government's overriding priority is to reduce taxes. The result is that people who were happy in and well suited to her home are being moved out to places which are cheaper. One of the reactions, she told me, was a move away from residential homes towards 'sheltered accommodation', because although the latter is often less suitable, it is exempt from the crippling regulations applied to residential homes.[121]

Evolution needed . . .

So there is a desperate need for the official mind also to be given cognitive fluidity. This would result in an immediate recognition of things that are already blindingly obvious to us humble folk on the ground, who have to operate the system.

But we are a long way from that goal. We are nowhere near the breakthrough which will be necessary to allow all of these different domains in the official mind to talk to one another automatically. The only hope we have of achieving the necessary cognitive fluidity in the over-mind is to use the cognitive fluidity that is a natural feature of the minds of individual people. Instead of denigrating and undermining the broad-based generalists among us, who have struggled to maintain their understanding and to retain their integrity and their feeling of responsibility to 'something beyond', we should be nurturing and treasuring them.

It is extremely hard work to maintain understanding. We need to encourage people to do it, not denigrate their attempts.

Our practice accountant says that he has seen this kind of change in his own field. When computerised systems were first introduced they were operated by people who had had experience of completing accounts ledgers by hand, as he had. So they had an understanding of what the systems were actually doing. The new generation knows all about computers, but it thinks that the answer to accounting problems involves feeding the right questions into the machine and pressing the right buttons (he actually uses the accountancy expression 'turning the handle', alluding to the old hand-cranked accounting machines).

It is not difficult to imagine problems arising when *nobody* knows how things actually work, and all of the expertise is in the machines. It is also not difficult to imagine that people with understanding will then be enormously in demand, but that we will have an immensely difficult job explaining to them why they should bother to make the necessary lifelong effort to maintain their understanding. Perhaps authority will find that it has sneered once too often at the goose that laid this golden egg.

UBM: understanding-based medicine

We need real doctors. Robo-doc will not be good enough. We need understanding-based medicine at least as much as evidence-based medicine, and probably a great deal more. This should be the next 'Big Idea'. We ought to be concentrating on ways to motivate people in the massive job of creating and maintaining their understanding. To do this we need to talk much less about power, control and hierarchy, and more about mutual respect.

We should be distinguishing explicitly between the advisory and the mandatory. Hints and tips are fine, appropriate and welcome, but 'Do thou this, or else' is not the way forward, if we as a society know what is good for us.

This lesson at least is simple. Where artificial models are tools to enhance human understanding they are good. Where they are used to *replace* human understanding they are bad.

The wrong kind of excellence

At the moment the system is simply unable to appreciate the kind of quality to which we on the front-line aspire – or our unwillingness to act down to the new standards and switch off our common sense and our integrity in the way that is now (unbelievably but quite explicitly) required.

It is the error of our age to impute to machines those automatic functions of our minds which we most take for granted. It is time to consider it possible that this approach may be wrong. Time to change priorities so that understanding-based actions, with their inherent imperfection and uncertainty, can trump actions based merely on the following of rules. Surely an enlightened society should see the abandonment of common sense in blind obedience to externally imposed rules as a crime. Instead of, as is the case today, the other way round.

The instinct is strong when we see a rule to switch off common sense and follow it like sheep. But the more we try to run the world without human understanding and insight, the more vulnerable we become. Some obstinately remain more responsible than this, but there is a terrible risk that eventually we shall all succumb, begin to do exactly what we are told, and *really* work to rule. Then heaven help us all.

> The wise man looks for answers in a book;
> But even fools know books can't understand.
> And recipes from Beryl Smith (the cook),
> However good, cannot taste salt from sand;
> And maps and charts which help you find your way
> Will not inform you where you want to go.
> And when you're lost inside a TV play
> It isn't there inside the box. And so
> You may be wise to look beyond the rule
> When taking doctor's orders to your heart;
> The source of understanding is life's school,
> Its teachers cannot play the robot's part.
>   While man 'anthropomorphs' each thing he sees,
>   Machines 'mechanomorph' the summer breeze.

CHAPTER THIRTEEN

Structure *v* Freedom

We are like battery hens . . . (in our old people's home) . . . I try to keep a bit free-range.

North America is a society which was constructed as an antidote to European civilisation . . . people went there to seek freedom . . . but now kids want some **rules***.*

Professor Michael Malus[122]

Freedom is about the willingness of every single human being to cede to lawful authority a great deal of discretion about what you do, and how you do it.

Rudy Giuliani, Mayor of New York City 1993–99[123]

'Techno-doc' or 'Robo-doc': an absolute distinction

I am tired of people like me being treated as dinosaurs[124] just because we don't leap with a glad cry and both feet into everything that is new and fashionable. In fact, as it happens, I am very close to being a techno-freak. I walk about with my pockets dragged out of shape by my mobile phone in my inside breast pocket, my Psion 3mx personal organiser in my left jacket pocket, my message-master pager clipped on to my belt, and my hard-wearing Filofax wallet, containing numerous plastic cards, in my right breast pocket. My right trouser pocket bulges with my high-tech keyring, which holds my key to unlock the car from a distance and my miniature Swiss army knife, which doesn't provide much defence against crocodiles, but is good for everything else.

At home I have so many tools, so many cameras, so many hi-fi and video devices and so many programs and peripherals for my computer that it would be embarrassing to list them. I even have an outside temperature and humidity gauge mounted on the wall by the back door.

In my consulting room I have a powerful computer with two printers, a noisy fan and a wonderful, flat screen which sits surprisingly neatly on the top of my old desk. It is connected to the practice server, to my partner's similar computer next door, to our reception desk and to our secretary. The receptionists check people in on their screen, and I can see on mine how many are waiting and how long it is since they arrived. Patients are often bemused by all of this hardware, but when a little beep sounds and I point out a message in the corner announcing 'T is served', they suddenly understand the point of it all.

The computer keeps the patients' records, of course, keeps track of prescriptions, automatically warns of interactions, and allows us to do all sorts of analyses. It also provides us with a host of look-up functions, including sophisticated expert systems and arrays of protocols. Yesterday (as I write) I saw a patient with shingles and was able to show him photographs of what a shingles rash can look like without treatment, and then to print out four pages of information for him to take away – two pages on shingles itself and two on post-herpetic neuralgia – because he was already getting the characteristic pain. All of this information is soundly based and well written, as I explained, and is regularly updated through the automatic telephone connection to the computer system provider. Then I was able to check the dosage and side-effects of the best available drug and print out the prescription, reusing the instructions that I had chosen carefully on a previous occasion.

When I need more help I have the CD-ROM version of the *Oxford Textbook of Medicine* ready to slip into the CD drive, and I have my filing cabinet and my two shelves of books, which also have their important uses.

None of this is quick, of course, and things break down when I am busy. Or when, as so often happens, the patient turns out to have a number of separate problems. However, that having been said, I think there can be no question that I, and thousands of GPs like me in the NHS, are just about the most technically empowered physicians that the world has ever known.

And, for the time being, we are free agents.

But people have other ideas. There are some who believe that protocols and expert systems should do *more* than give advice. They believe that they should tell doctors what to do. The National Institute for Clinical Excellence has stated, and repeated, that doctors who diverge from its guidelines should write down in the patients' notes their reasons for doing so, on every occasion. This marks a shift, and it is a shift which is absolute, from guidelines as *advice* to guidelines as *rules*.

It is but a short step from this to every divergence from guidelines becoming *prima facie* evidence of malpractice, automatically indefensible in law, which I suppose might be fine if medicine could be defined in rules . . .

For me this change is unacceptable – *absolutely* unacceptable. I do not and will not write down my reasons on every occasion that I diverge from standard guidelines. If this is going to make it impossible for me to remain in practice, then I will not do so. To pretend that any such stipulation is practicable is to collude with the Utopian illusion. I have convinced myself, if I have convinced no one else, that this would be completely wrong. I have also convinced myself that it would mean I was no longer a doctor.

Yes . . . Yes . . . Yes . . .

Two summers ago I got round to reading James Joyce's *Ulysses*. I had read George Eliot's *Middlemarch* a few years earlier because it was 'the best novel ever written', and was rather inclined to agree that it might be, but then I saw somewhere that *Ulysses* was the best novel ever written as well. So, not to be outdone, when I saw that the Folio Society was producing a nice edition, I ordered it. It took me a while, but I read every word.

People say that they find *Ulysses* difficult to read because it hasn't any structure, and it was therefore a surprise for me to find that it was a *showcase* of structure, a *celebration* of structure. It has layer upon layer of structure, yet the whole thing adds up to a glorious affirmation of the richness of life. That is the opinion of my tennis-partner, Michael, a brilliant actor/director in Lesley's drama group, an Aston Villa supporter, man of letters and Roman Catholic priest.

That is the opinion of a Scandinavian speaker at a medical conference who by coincidence held up his copy just when I was at the half-way point in my reading (I had my own copy with me at the conference as bedside reading) and called it 'The greatest novel ever written'. Yes, a *Scandinavian* – that is the opinion of the world.

Let me attempt to explain why. James Joyce puts the whole of life into one man's journey through one day, and into one journey through the heart of Dublin, which of course tourists retrace every day. He uses a succession of brilliantly parodied styles, as if he is also putting the whole of literature into one book. Now we are reading a medieval epic, now we are reading the script of a play, now we are reading a seedy pot-boiler, now we are in a long chapter composed entirely of clichés – I counted nine in one sentence – and so the variety goes on and on. Dazzling.

The famous 30-odd pages of unpunctuated stream of consciousness at the end – yes, difficult to read, but worth it – yes, yes, yes – is but one of a fabulously rich sampler of literary styles. And behind all this we learn that there lies another structure, which I hardly saw at all because I lacked the necessary classical background. Every scene is matched to a scene from Homer's *Odyssey*. Joyce's central character is Everyman; Homer's hero is Ulysses. QED.

Unsuitable to the genius of a free nation

Bill Bryson, who wrote the popular book *Notes From a Small Island*, is less well known as an authority on linguistics. In his delightful account of the English language, *Mother Tongue*,[125] he provides remarkable insights into the stultifying effects of official attempts to regularise language. Dryden in 1664, Defoe in 1697, Swift in 1712 and John Adams in 1780 all urged regularisation of English and especially its spelling. Together they contributed to pressure for a regulatory body in this country along the lines of the Académie Française founded by Cardinal Richelieu in 1635.

Bryson points to 'the one almost inevitable shortcoming of national academies. However progressive and farseeing they may be to begin with, they almost always exert over time a depressive effect on change ...' Samuel Johnson and Thomas Jefferson spoke against the idea of such regulation, while 'Joseph Priestley, the English scientist, grammarian and theologian, spoke perhaps most eloquently against the formation of an academy when he said in 1761 that it was "unsuitable to the genius of a free nation"'.

Thanks to this resistance the English language is now 'often commended by outsiders for its lack of a stultifying authority'.

We should be grateful that some of our ancestors in this island were dinosaurs.

Love is blind

Lesley and I are in the car with Michael on the way to see a play at Newbury's wonderful little Watermill Theatre. We are taking the opportunity to practise for our own imminent production of some of Shakespeare's songs. We are going to do 14 of them, from different plays, in a variety of arrangements, each set in a scene based on a page or so of its surrounding dialogue. Michael will be singing Schubert's 'Who is Sylvia?', and as we drive up the A34 in the brilliant sunshine we are playing the accompaniment tape on the car system and singing together to help him memorise the words. Michael then remarks that he finds it difficult to make sense of the words in the second verse: 'Is she kind as she is fair, for beauty lives in kindness. Love does to her eyes repair to help him of his blindness, and being helped inhabits there.'

'Sounds like gibberish', I agree. Then I start musing about how I get used to things not making sense in my life as a GP. So little of the medicine I see adds up to any sort of clear picture or clear diagnosis. Still less often do I get a clear cure. I seem to go through life accepting that most things are fuzzy, just as I accept that the town is full of faces I know that I know but which I cannot place. I have got so used to this that it doesn't even worry me much any more. I just smile and say 'hello', and most of the time it is fine. I read poetry in rather the same way (when I do read poetry, that is), letting it wash over me and not bothering to work out precisely what it is all supposed to mean. Making a virtue, now I come to think of it, of recognising that if the poet had been able to give what he was saying one precise meaning he wouldn't have written a poem. If he could have tied the whole thing up neatly in a clever *bottom line* he would have done precisely that. And that wasn't because he wasn't clever. Surely no one who has spent time reading Shakespeare can have any doubt about the consummate genius of the man.

So we drive on and I start singing to myself again, 'Love does to her eyes repair to help him of his blindness' and suddenly it clicks: *Love is blind*. That's it. 'Him' means Love, the God of Love. Love decides to use Sylvia's eyes 'to help him of his blindness'. And, having 'repaired' to her eyes (i.e. moved in) he decides to stay – '... and being helped, inhabits there' – to enjoy the view, presumably.

So Sylvia's eyes have Love, in person, living inside them, which I now see is an extremely nice thing to say about Sylvia, not to mention her eyes, and justifies the extremity of hyperbole in the final verse: 'she exceeds each mortal thing upon the dull earth dwelling, to her let us garlands bring.'

'OK, the basic shape of a sonnet is easy. Different people did it in different ways, but this is the way Shakespeare did it ...' Judith moves her tea cup to make a space on our sitting-room table and spreads out a sheet of paper, just as she does for A-level students at the college. This is our personal lesson, at the beginning of my six months off. Because I had said I was interested in the way you can get freedom within rigid structures such as sonnet form. Something like that.

The rhyme form is easy, she tells us. The first line rhymes with the third, and the second rhymes with the fourth – ABAB. Then repeat, with new rhymes, for the fifth and seventh, sixth and eighth and then again for the ninth and eleventh and tenth and twelfth – CDCD EFEF. Then finish off with a rhyming couplet at the end – GG. Fourteen lines in all – ABAB CDCD EFEF GG. The metre is straightforward: de dum de dum de dum de dum de dum – Shall I compare thee to a summer's day? This is the *iambic pentameter* of dimly remembered lessons on English literature.

Right, now for the meaning. That first line poses the question, and the second begins to answer it: 'Thou art **more** lovely and **more** temperate' (i.e. you are not at all like a summer's day). 'Rough winds do shake the darling buds of May, And summer's lease hath all too short a date' (summer is pretty awful sometimes, and anyway it's soon over). Now Shakespeare begins to build up his argument, like a debater: *this* and *this*, and then again *this*. 'Sometimes too hot the eye of heaven shines' (sometimes it's too hot), 'And often is his gold complexion dimmed' (and sometimes it's dreary), 'And every fair from fair sometime declines' (every beautiful thing will lose its beauty in time), 'By chance or nature's changing course untrimmed' (course, untrimmed – you trim sails to a course – we are talking sailing here, Judith; even if chance events don't destroy beauty, however cleverly you steer you can't deny nature forever).

Now we get to a completely new idea: 'But thy **eternal** summer shall **not** fade, Nor lose possession of that fair thou ow'st' ('ow'st' is an old usage – the beauty you *possess* will not fade, as the beauty of nature does). 'Nor shall death brag thou wander'st in his shade'. What a *wonderful* use of words. Nor shall death *brag . . .* (death swaggering about and *bragging* that he is going to get us in the end). 'Nor shall death brag, thou wander'st in his shade, When in eternal lines to time thou grow'st'. Suddenly we begin to see, and the final couplet, in what is called the 'turn',[126] swings the whole thing round, so that we discover the pearl of deeper meaning: 'So long as men can breathe, or eyes can see, So long lives this, and this gives life to thee.' That's the point – *this* is the sonnet itself. Shakespeare is saying that it is his *poem*, not his beloved, that is immortal, but that through his poem his beloved is in a sense immortal, too.

Impossible to convey the enthusiasm, the love, the inspiration of the way Judith tells this – the privilege. Impossible to prescribe, impossible to pin down and formulate. Precious and irreplaceable.

We speak of 'capturing' thoughts in words, but they can also gently cradle an idea and set it free. The wrong kind of structure can make a prison for our lives, but without structure it is impossible for us to live at all.

We'll start the meeting now at Section A,
Which, kindly note, I've subdivided twice.
And at A2 I'll have a word to say
About sub-section 4. It would be nice
To get the business through by half past four
So, comments brief, and make them through the chair
Or else . . . And Section B could be a bore
But where it's coming from I'd like to share
Before we get to grips with Section C.
The PowerPoint should help to make that clear,
For which we thank our secretary, Dee.
So – if you'd read the minutes for us, dear –
   This meeting is to settle policy:
   'To AOB, or not to AOB?'

CHAPTER FOURTEEN

OK, so what . . .?

'Thank you for everything you did, and your team'

First stanza: the statement of the problem

'It's a funny thing, they were all very good, but he kept asking for Doctor Willis.'

It was one of the shocks when I got back to work after my six-month sabbatical. Only a month earlier (I was told) he had gone in for tests for a stomach pain and the exploratory operation had found pancreatic cancer spreading right through the organs of his upper abdomen. There was no possibility of removing it, and they had just closed up the incision knowing that he was dying. Now at home – because he had hated it in hospital and his wife had insisted – already in the last stages. On a syringe-driver,[127] nurses going in several times a day, and a night nurse most nights. Everything nicely under control, with the team in full swing. The National Health Service at its best.

I offered to do the visit that was due on that first Monday I was back, drove the five miles in the sunshine, found the front door open and walked into the empty hallway. 'Hello . . .' I called.

'Come on up, please.' The familiar voice from the landing – she sees who I am as I come up the stairs. I take her hand and we just look at each other for a moment. Then she shows me in.

'It's Doctor Willis, dear . . . come to see you.'

I don't do anything. Really, there is nothing *to* do. I bring up a chair and sit down, thinking, remembering, saying something. 'What a beautiful airy room. With the sun streaming in from the common like that. I've hardly ever been here, have I? Your garden is superb.'

He had been so pleased with his new hip, before I went away. When he had finally got it, after all the waiting, after I'd written to say how bravely he was putting up with the pain, asking the consultant to give him some priority, saying how much he wanted to get back to a little golf. The National Health Service at its worst.

Then I think of the rest of the long, long saga. All of the years since they moved to the area and joined my list. We always got on well. He had a lot of problems with different joints, and a maddeningly difficult gout which would never do the right things with what should have been the right treatment. Old friends, really. I open up his notes on my knee and write something, just for the record.

'Have you finished the book, then?' He looks thin, and incredibly older, but also incredibly the same.

'Well, not quite, but I think I'm getting somewhere. I've had a brilliant time.'

His wife sees me looking at a striking photograph on the wall, 'That's one of his.'

'Really? It's superb.' I look back at him and I can see he is pleased.

'The next room is full of his photographs.'

'Really? Can I see? I never knew.'

It *is* full of his photographs, and cameras, and boxes of equipment. All of the walls covered with portraits, girls' faces mainly. 'He got known and he took everybody, he just loved doing it.' Easy to see why he got known. Some amateur! I look back into his room on my way to the stairs.

'Your photographs are superb.' Definitely the thing to say.

Next day he is sinking fast and two days later he is dead.

A month later she is here to see me in surgery, as she promised. Telling me how busy she is, sorting everything out. All the things she has to do. How the house seems so empty.

'I thought I might get a dog.'

'Yes, that's a wonderful idea. You must get a dog. Something alive in the house.'

She hesitates after opening the door, looking back.

'Come again if I can help. Yes, get a dog . . .'

It almost seemed that it was *meant* for me to get back three days before he died. Of course it wasn't really, but I'm sure he would have understood the point. He was certainly one of the hundreds of patients with whom I explored these ideas in my consulting room over the years. And now, as I try to picture us talking there, I fancy I can remember him commenting on my own photographs on the walls. Yes, I'm sure I can.

The point I'm so sure he would have understood is this: none of this *counts*. None of it registers on the 'performance indicators' of the new way of doing things. To the official mind none of this matters. It is completely invisible.

And yet you know, I know, he knows, his wife knows, my wife knows – everybody knows – that these human things are really the things that matter *most* in the end. That is the extent of the gulf, that is the scale of the problem. The two cultures. The two sides of the world. Each oblivious to the other, permeating each other utterly, yet hardly interacting at all. Like neutrinos, elementary particles that stream through space and straight through the heart of our planet, without affecting it, or being affected *by* it, in the smallest degree.

As I give this chapter its final form, I am oppressed by the intractability of the problem I am addressing. At work I find respected friends and colleagues, almost without exception, regarding increased regulation and control of doctors as inevitable. 'We don't like it, but that's the way it's going', is what they say. 'He who pays the piper calls the tune.' And from so many contemporaries, seeing themselves as the lucky ones, those awful, 'cop-out' words, 'Roll on retirement.'

And the executive, meanwhile, so far from seeing the problem, has only just begun. It sees regulation, without any shadow of self-doubt, as the very embodiment of progress, and it wants much more of it.

The National Health Service Plan of July 2000[128] talks of 'arm's-length control' and then says, 'Doctors, therapists and nurses will increasingly work to standard protocols'.[129] It talks about 'earned autonomy', and then explains that this means 'green-light organisations' having fewer of the new official checks than 'red-light organisations', with 'yellow-light organisations' somewhere in between. A hospital manager friend tells me that they are already being audited to death and that he seriously doubts the capacity of the system to accommodate the apparatus of additional procedures now proposed.

And so the thing goes on, and everyone can see the problem, and no one can see the problem. We are being sucked into the vortex, and there is a feeling of real anger, of real grievance, as I see the way that the humanity of good people is being usurped and squandered. But the devil of it is that I can see both sides of this, and so can we all. It is more important than ever to answer the question I started with: *how on earth can two such vastly different views of life be reconciled?*

Second stanza: developing the answer

Part of my answer is that the official view simply does not accept the validity of the kind of evidence it ought to be taking into account.

When Radcliffe Hall was accused of obscenity for her book, *The Well of Loneliness*, George Bernard Shaw and a number of other great literary figures of the day came forward to defend her at her trial. But they weren't allowed to speak. The judge ruled their evidence inadmissible. He said they weren't competent to talk about obscenity (presumably one of his own areas of expertise), and that was that. Their famous voices remained unheard.

It is the same when we try to articulate the front-line view of life, in which relative values and feelings are of such importance. The official mind can only register the measurable and the fixed. Some of the most important considerations, which we take into account automatically in our personal judgements, are inadmissible evidence on the official scale. Evidence that doesn't follow the rules, that is not submitted on the necessary form, that doesn't count. In vain do we protest that that is exactly the point: please listen – we are talking here about things that *can't be counted*. The system is completely blind to the problem. It is *shouting* at everyone else, but the official mind can't see it at all. The scattered voices, Lesley's and mine among them, remain unheard.

And although we can all see it from both points of view, when we have to choose one of the points of view as a basis for our actual decisions, however strong our instincts and our feelings to the contrary, when we are operating in the official side of life, it is the hard, fixed, quantified point of view which wins. There is no contest and no discussion. The other course cannot possibly be justified, because it is not, by its very nature, open to justification.

The question is how to obtain some sort of purchase, some sort of leverage – how to *connect*. That is the reason I have dwelt so obsessively on the subject of authority. Little of what I am saying is new. These things are the common currency of daily conversations, probably all over the world. But on the official level, all over the world, they are utterly discounted. They do not register at all. We are not just speaking a different language, but a different *kind* of language. In vain do we hammer on the bolted shutters of 'their' minds.

Oliver Cromwell expressed his frustration against the perennial arrogance of the official view in his vivid sentence: 'I beseech you, in the bowels of Christ, think it possible you may be mistaken'.[130] Not the words I would have chosen myself, but I share the sentiment exactly. Think it *possible* – that is the key. Think it possible that we are not simply dealing here with ideas which are being abused or applied with too much enthusiasm. Think it possible that the ideas are *fundamentally misguided* and quite simply wrong.

Take that apparently knock-out saying, 'He who pays the piper calls the tune'. Think it possible for a moment that the conventional meaning is nonsense.

It seems to me that anyone who employs a piper would be a fool to tell him what to play. Pay him well, by all means, although it would be sensible to do that afterwards. But for goodness' sake let him choose his own tunes. I counsel this most strongly, come to think of it. And as for trying to operate his lungs, his mouth and his fingers like a puppet, do I need to spell out the stupidity of that? Well, yes, come to think of it, in this context perhaps I do.

There we are, isn't it amazing? *Coup de grâce* to *own goal* in an instant. The conventional meaning revealed as an empty mantra, by a moment's scepticism. If you are paying a piper you leave the guy to get on with it in as much freedom as you can possibly devise. You know it makes sense.

I have a dream, which is expressed in George Eliot's line:

> *If we had a keen vision and feeling of all ordinary human life, it would be like hearing the grass grow and the squirrel's heart beat, and we should die of that roar which lies on the other side of silence.*[131]

My dream is that the world will begin to listen to the scattered voices, that the curtain will lift and the deafening roar will be heard at last.

In a nutshell, I think we have got it wrong about the nature of reality. We need a new understanding which is simply more sophisticated than hitherto. Major new modes of perception have always needed new frames of understanding. Few changes in history have equalled the one that our generation has experienced. It would be surprising if our old models were adequate to reflect faithfully our new, fabulously enhanced perspective. And while we continue to use the old models the madness will continue.

We have *raised our gaze*, and this applies in a thousand ways. It is as if the optician has given us seven-league contact lenses, acting like immensely powerful binoculars, and forgotten to tell us he has done so. Thus equipped, we clump our booted feet among the egg-shell problems of our daily lives, our eyes fixed on what we assume to be a higher view.

We see before us a magnificent, horizonless vista of what we assume to be reality, but it is in fact an highly artificial construct, generalised up from unimaginably small elements, which are chosen at best at random and all too often because they are *unusual*. And without the background subconscious appreciation of the whole picture which we take for granted in our unaided perception, generalisations from the exceptional and incongruous (i.e. scare-stories and headlines) give us a distorted and corrupted picture.

Not only do we use technology in this way to extend our view, but also society as a whole uses it to construct models from that information. The tools include words, statistics, mathematics, computer spreadsheets, photographs and clay. And just as technology corrupts the information that we receive, it also corrupts the model of reality which society holds in common in its 'over-mind'.

Some of the corruption occurs because the over-mind unwittingly amplifies the *failings* of the natural mind. Characteristics which are mere peccadilloes on the personal scale are blown up into massive distortions and illusions when translated to the artificial model. The lure of the new, the fixed and the absolute. Our inability to judge the relative importance of finite risks. Our inability to call off the endless hunt for perfection. The over-mind resembles a patient with obsessive-compulsive disorder, performing endless checking rituals, yet without the insight which so often accompanies (although notoriously it does not help) this crippling complaint.

Equally importantly, the over-mind unwittingly lacks the *strengths* of the natural mind. In particular, the phenomenal power of our natural minds to model the *whole* of our experience, and to keep it in constant interaction with the infinitesimal fraction which will fit into our conscious attention at any particular time, is something which has no counterpart in the artificial over-mind at all.

Front-line generalists recognise this better, perhaps, than most, because it is our job to deal in wholes. So many of the things which we perceive as unchallengeable sense, when we view them one part at a time, jump out as obvious madness, like the hidden images in the stereograms which were in vogue some years ago, when we let our eyes go out of focus and see the whole.

So here is another linking feature which goes some way further towards solving our puzzle. It is that in each case the madness is only apparent when we look at the whole, and it is completely invisible when we look at its parts. This makes the madness invisible to an overmind which prides itself on basing everything on its clever reductionist tools.

So we are wrong to ascribe to our senses and minds the characteristics of machines, and we are wrong to ascribe to machines the characteristics of our senses and minds. But that is not enough. If it had all been as simple as that, I would have written a much simpler book. It wouldn't have needed any poetical allusions, that's for sure. Something much deeper and much more radical is needed to complete this puzzle. Something like the following.

Third stanza (the 'turn'): a new way of seeing things

We pride ourselves on being rational animals, yet when we look closely we manifestly are not so. But, despite our assumptions to the contrary, our irrationality is more of a strength than a weakness. Indeed our irrationality is essential. The time has come to stop being apologetic for it.

Because, although we assume that we live in a rational world, when we look closely we manifestly do not. Our minds have evolved in response to that reality. Our problems arise when we pretend that reality is rational or, as Penrose puts it, 'computable', and when we assume that our minds ought to be rational in order to model it properly.

Looked at this way, the rationality into which not only computers but *all of the machines and systems of rules we can ever construct* are irrevocably locked is making our problems much, much worse. Because, while we use machines and systems more and more to model reality, they are in fact incapable of doing this with the reliability and accuracy which we believe to be their unique strength.

It is difficult to imagine a better setting in which to model this clash (between art and science is one way of putting it) than general practice. Battling through a busy surgery, saving lives with both hands, as we say, every patient having more and more problems however deeply we look, and every problem having more and more layers of complexity, it is as obvious as anything could be that we are doing something which is beyond computation. Bits of it are, of course, but computing the whole thing at once is impossible.

However, this truth is very far from obvious to the outsider. The outsider is enthralled by the power and sophistication of his new modelling tools, and he knows that every aspect of our work that he looks at could be done better by using them. He sees it as only a matter of time before our entire role will be reduced to a formula, and every situation we deal with will have a single, correct answer.

In the past this was a theoretical question of no practical importance, but now the tools are with us, which makes it a very practical question indeed. The new tools have forced a confrontation with the problem, and the cracks are opening wide. Say 'Ah.'

The failure of the architects of the Millennium Thames foot-bridge to predict that it would wobble dangerously when people walked across it might perhaps have lessened public confidence, but there is little sign that it has done so. Here was a carefully planned structure made of materials whose physical properties are known with great precision, which was presumably designed using the most sophisticated computer simulations available by people who knew exactly what they were trying to prevent, namely a wobble when people walked across it. And despite all of this they got their answer completely wrong. The bridge was closed for an indefinite period one day after its opening.

At the same time, in another part of London, the Department of Health was pressing on with its programme of audits, protocols and information systems, with the promise that it will eliminate error in the unimaginably greater complexity of the health provision of the entire nation. Hubris entirely undiminished.

It may be true to say that every bridge failure and every aircraft crash ought to be preventable. Although even that is questionable, and in the case of boats at sea it is generally accepted that freak waves, with massively tall, vertical, breaking faces will occur that are capable of sinking a boat of almost any size. Such monsters are described as non-negotiable.[132] Human things are different, not just quantitatively but also qualitatively, not just in extent but also in kind. Not every death is preventable in medicine, and good deaths are among our most tangible successes.

Our generation has experienced a change in view comparable to the ones which led to the Copernican revolution, the Darwinian revolution, relativity and quantum mechanics.

We have started using new tools which have brought a revelation that something doesn't fit. The record we are so diligently assembling simply doesn't make sense, because it is being composed of corrupted data that are being compiled in a corrupted way. And, just as might be expected, the first people to see the problem are generalists working on the front-line whose job it is to make the thing work as a whole.

The corruption runs deep. Our age is characterised by a quite extraordinary dominance of the executive over the people who actually do things. The Cambrian explosion of doctor-regulating bodies at the end of the twentieth century speaks of desperation, a fad, a cult, of a playground craze. But the even more extraordinary thing is that the people who actually do things largely acquiesce to this. Even in our proudly democratic culture, we display the 'serf mentality' which Václav Havel bemoaned as a characteristic of the Russian people.[133]

We seem no longer to trust the evidence of our own eyes and our own judgement. Technical hubris has brought with it nemesis for the personal aspects of life. We have experienced a massive loss of confidence in our human abilities. Everywhere these abilities have been replaced by system. The popular perception of computers is that they have destroyed people's jobs, but the situation is much worse than that. They have usurped and humbled our humanity and left us with little reason for being here. And we are being told that this change is inevitable – it is progress, it is the future. Worse than that, we are telling *ourselves* these things. We are abdicating our birthright, and we are doing it willingly, with a smile.

And the whole thing is based on a misunderstanding, a false belief that the world can be sorted out for good – a gigantic simultaneous equation solved for the millennium. The end of history. The end of science. Aren't we clever...?

The new understanding is that life is not a simultaneous equation, however much logic tells us that it ought to be. It has no single solution, however intricate and beautiful we believe that solution could be.

Our lives have opened out into two parallel and utterly disparate paths. We are moving forward in two ways which cannot be formally reconciled. Structure and freedom, the fixed and the fuzzy, the professional and the amateur, the modern and the postmodern. Two by two they walk along. The specialist and the generalist, the game and the life, the virtual and the reality, the 'them' and the 'us'. Somehow we need to link these paired hands with the magic of balance and respect. And that can only be done with the vital ingredient *mystery*, which classical science denies. And it also has to be done without denying classical science.

It seems a ridiculous idea – as ridiculous as matter being made of waves and particles but never of both at once. But that mystery is something which classical science tells us is true.

So try this ridiculous idea for size. Perhaps, at last, rigid, classical thinking has reached the end of its two and a half thousand year tenure. Perhaps our new confrontation with the profound mystery of reality is going to force nothing less than an historic accommodation with romantic philosophy, from which classical philosophy diverged in ancient Greece.

If new ideas do not seem ridiculous, they seem dangerous. The inquisitors who forced Galileo to recant his discoveries probably feared chaos would descend, and that the dark ages would return, if their orthodoxy was overturned. But the Earth stubbornly continued on its course around the Sun, refusing to be at the centre of the universe as the inquisitors would have preferred. Chaos did not descend, and instead mankind moved on to a higher understanding.

Today science is our defence against the mysticism, mumbo-jumbo and pseudoscience which are such paradoxical features of our supposedly scientific age. Medicine provides particularly clear examples of this phenomenon. But although it might easily appear that doubting the computability of nature is playing into the hands of this dangerous anti-science and threatening chaos, in fact it is nothing of the kind. Nor did the acceptance of the bizarre uncertainty of quantum mechanics represent a capitulation to irrationality. Truth, stranger indeed than fiction, cannot forever be denied. What is more, moving on to a more sophisticated understanding is the legitimate way to spike the guns of those who reject the whole of science because they find that the present orthodoxy leaves undeniable parts of their experience unexplained.

Just before I started my study leave, Christopher Everett lent me a book written by a Second World War fighter pilot, Richard Hillary, who was shot down during the Battle of Britain. It was quite clearly written as a kind of therapy during his recovery from a long succession of plastic surgery operations for terrible burns to his face which he suffered while escaping from his blazing cockpit. It was called *The Last Enemy*, and it enjoyed great popularity in the post-war years. Another classic.

The following passage describes an incident when Hillary and a fellow pilot who had been up at Oxford with him were alone in a railway compartment. They were travelling south to fetch two new Spitfires for their squadron, which was based at Montrose in Scotland. The friend, Peter, whom the author paints as an extraordinarily admirable young man, certainly the hero of the book, who was killed a few days later, reluctantly tried to put into words his private reasons for believing in the war:

> *I don't know if I can answer you to your satisfaction, but I'll try. I would say that I was fighting the war to rid the world of fear − of the fear of fear is perhaps what I mean. If the Germans win this war, nobody except little Hitlers will dare do anything. England will be run as if it were a concentration camp, or at best a factory. All courage will die out of the world − the courage to love, to create, to take risks, whether physical or intellectual or moral. Men will hesitate to carry out the promptings of the heart or the brain because, having acted, they will live in fear that their action may be discovered and themselves cruelly punished. Thus all love, all spontaneity, will die out of the*

world. Emotion will have atrophied. Thought will have petrified. The oxygen breathed by the soul, so to speak, will vanish, and mankind will wither. Does that satisfy you? [134]

This passage made my spine tingle. Here was a voice from the dead – from a generation of young men who died to prevent the things happening that are worrying me so much today. But now we walk with open arms, with a welcoming smile, towards the danger that they saw, and only a few of us seem to feel the fear any more.[135]

Final couplet

I know that readers who have read this far will be in two minds about my message. In fact they will be in three, but I suspect that the third mind – the under-mind – accepted a great deal of my argument from the start.

So it is the other two minds that I am addressing as I begin to state what I think we ought to do. First, the individual consciousness of the reader, and secondly, the over-mind, in which in this strange, total yet partial way we all share. Individuals reacted to my first book by saying, 'Yes, we can see what you are saying, but what can we do about it? Is there anything better than simply saying "No"?' And I got no reaction from the over-mind at all. This time I am hoping to do better on both counts.

Of course society is inherently resistant to change and suspicious of anything really new. This is entirely right and proper, otherwise no society would last for very long. But where totalitarian states tend to silence their dissident voices, we ignore them, which is more genteel and more effective. Even so, the fact that our society sub-scribes, at least officially, to the rule of rational argument is the Achilles' heel of ossified dogma. It gives the individual a precious chance to influence the over-mind. The question 'What is the pro-blem you are trying to solve?', for example, is a litmus test for the exposure of empty process. Time and again this simple question, asked in child-like innocence at solemn meetings, will reveal that resources are being devoted to the sterile implementation of *plans*, weighty in every sense, which parted long ago from the human problems that they were once intended to address. It is a case of doing the model, extravagantly crafted though it may be, instead of the thing.

Similarly, it is often helpful to ask to be shown the evidence that a particular innovation has been proved to be safe. After all, a society which demands evidence-based actions on the periphery can reasonably be expected to have implemented them first at the centre. Unless, that is, the executive exempts itself from its own rules.

And then, of course, we can indeed say 'no'. If we believe that what we are being told to do is wrong we have no choice. But it helps a lot if we say no together.

Finally, we can be more confident of our human abilities, proud of our balance, and refuse to be labelled or stereotyped. When the seductive voice on the television advertisement urges us to 'refuse to compromise', we can say, 'Rubbish, that is a recipe for anarchy'. When it goes on, 'You *can* come *first*', we can ask, 'Do you really mean *all* of us?'

Life in the round is not a football match, or a war, or a formalised debate; we do not give our support wholly to one side or the other. We have broken our primitive allegiance to the tribe. Against our animal instincts we give our support somewhere in the middle ground, and all our discussion is about positioning the balance. Nor does this make us traitors to either cause, but rather it makes us worthy of the maturity of the human race.

And so to the over-mind. If you want the reason, in one sound bite, why this book is unlikely to influence the over-mind, then I would say that it is because the over-mind can only understand sound bites. Our common consciousness is blind to the kind of joined up argument I have been obliged to use.

But it isn't as simple as that, and I shall imagine for a moment that my point has indeed gone home, and that we recognise our present course is based on a wrong paradigm, an outdated understanding of the way in which reality operates. That we see how much we depend on conscientious, resourceful, free individuals, and how dangerous and naive it is to think that we can dispense with them and let the ship sail into the future on autopilot, with nobody on board, like the *Marie Celeste*. In that improbable case, the following is what we should do.

Put humanity back at the centre of things, at the heart. We must not let society become too complex and too automatic for people to understand. We must keep it within our comprehension. It is worth making huge sacrifices in terms of crude efficiency to achieve this.

Back off with all the rules and give people space to breathe. Much more than we think. Much more than we would like. The object of rules should be to define the limits of acceptable behaviour, not to specify the details.[136] Tell people not to kill each other, of course, and enforce that law as rigorously as we can, but don't try to tell them when to brush their teeth. And for people to use rules in order to satisfy their personal lust for power should be as unacceptable as the indulgence of any other animal lust at the expense of others. That is what civilisation is there to protect us from, if civilisation is to be worthy of the name.

Give people a reason for living and they will rise to the challenge. We hear a lot about irresponsible, spoilt children these days, but Dickens caught the truth of the way in which children rise to a challenge in his character the Artful Dodger. The same is grimly obvious in accounts of street children in Rio, and the same is sublimely obvious in the professionalism of child-choristers in cathedral choirs.

I am thinking of a husband who looks after his wife who has Alzheimer's dementia, one of a number I have known well. We hear a lot about the uncaringness of modern husbands, but what I see is selfless dedication, year after year, to the point of physical and emotional exhaustion. I see humour and humanity shining through:

Thanks for coming up so quick the other day. No, I really means it. After fifty-something years you kind of gets used to them. Though I often say I didn't have a grey hair when I first knew her.

Start looking at these real people and stop basing actions on the exceptions.

If we take away the challenge, the importance of daily actions, the feeling that people can make a difference, we do so at our peril.

I see general practice as a precious example of a particular way of doing things. It has been a close-run thing, but despite everything, despite being thought to be 'history', we GPs do still exist.[137] We have to be inclusive. We cannot say, 'That is not my field'. In an age when people are increasingly refusing to accept any risks at all, GPs, like other front-line workers, quietly take risks *all the time*. We have to work with the constant knowledge that operating to the standard expected of us by society, in particular by the courts, is not merely impossible, but that any attempt to do so would enormously harm the patients we have to help. All this should, in any sensible scheme of things, give us considerable authority.

Modern doctors have moved beyond the days when everyone had to be sent away with a bottle of medicine. A great many of our patients go away without a prescription these days. We recognise that there are many occasions when doing nothing is the best, although often the most difficult, treatment to prescribe.

People in high places would do well to look closely at this model, instead of rejecting it as obsolete. Just as doctors have learned better than to prescribe 'a pill for every ill', so legislators ought not pass a *bill* for every ill. They should be like sophisticated GPs, who really do 'play God' – they grant their patients free will. God, or nature, or both, draws back from telling people exactly what to do, that much is clear. Not just because that is a nice way to treat people, but because telling people exactly what to do *doesn't work*. The job of the executive, so beautifully allegorised in the book of Genesis, is to give people free will, to set the margins of life as widely as possible, and to allow the maximum space for human flourishing.

We shall know things are improving when we see fewer rules, not more, when we see forms getting smaller rather than continually longer, when we see the courts tempering their expectation of perfection, and when we see every species of personal initiative, in its glorious diversity, being welcomed in our society. Then we can grow, with a new, more sophisticated understanding of the mystery of reality, into the full richness of life – a life immeasurably enhanced and protected, instead of being enslaved, by modern technology.

There is something *beyond* our brave, new, proxy, second-hand, virtual reality which is what it's all about. Some vital ingredient which turns the game into life, but which is invisible, can't be pinned down, can't be defined, can't be controlled, can't be demanded – can't be replaced. And it is down here, in the low places of life.

> '*So what are you writing about?*'
>> '*Well, I'm waiting to hear from a publisher. But it's about the fact that people are more important than systems. People are what life is all about.*'
> '*That's really interesting. That's so important. I should like to see that. Let me know when it's out . . .*'

References

1 Fish D and Coles C (1997) *Developing Professional Judgement in Health Care*. Butterworth-Heinemann, Oxford.
2 Under the terms of service of the National Health Service, a GP is allowed one period of extended study leave in his or her career, but has to obtain approval in advance for the chosen project.
3 Quoted with permission.
4 General practice was very unfashionable in those days. My medical school, the Middlesex, boasted of the small proportion of its output of doctors that became GPs. I was the only student in my year who arranged personal experience of general practice or declared any intention of becoming a GP.
5 Goodman N (1999) *British Journal of General Practice*. **March**: 255. 'I found myself surrounded by public health doctors. My *BMJ* stayed firmly out of sight and an interesting train journey it turned out to be . . . To describe their attitude to coalface doctors (i.e. doctors who see patients) as one of barely concealed contempt would be untrue: their attitude was one of outright contempt. To them, coalface doctors wasted public money and needed whipping into line.'
6 My friend, John Lane, who was a pharmacist in Stony Stratford when I was a GP there in 1971, remembers that this was the standard answer given at the time to patients who asked for the name of the tablets they had been given. It was only in 1972 that it became normal for drugs to be labelled with their contents.
7 Reserpine did not cause depression directly. The suicides associated with it were probably related to the horrible side-effect of akathisia, a kind of jumpiness.
8 As a matter of fact, my relationship with this patient never did fully recover from this incident, and a few months later I discovered that she had transferred to the list of a neighbouring doctor.
9 ESR = erythrocyte sedimentation rate. Red blood cells slowly settle in a column of anticoagulated blood. If there is a lot of immunological activity in the blood, the cells clump together and sink more quickly. This

simple test is a useful pointer to some types of inflammatory illnesses. The normal value is below 10 mm/hour.

10 HRT = hormone replacement therapy, i.e. oestrogen replacement for menopausal symptoms.

11 Diamorphine (heroin) is regarded as the drug of choice to control pain during terminal illnesses in the UK and Canada. All other countries ban it because of fears that it will induce addiction. This is one reason why I want to die in the UK.

12 Leading article, *The Independent*, 12 May 1999.

13 Dyson F (1997) *Imagined Worlds.* Harvard University Press, Cambridge, MA. Dyson challenges the idea that revolutions are driven almost exclusively by new concepts. This idea he attributes to a book by Thomas Kuhn, *The Structure of Scientific Revolutions*, which talked almost exclusively about concepts and hardly at all about tools. This brilliantly written book became a classic and 'misled a whole generation of students and historians of science into believing that all scientific revolutions are concept-driven'. Dyson lists during the last 500 years only six major concept-driven revolutions, as opposed to some *20* tool-driven revolutions.

14 www.thebrain.com

15 As I complete my run-through of the final manuscript, a year after this section was first written, the number stands at 3805.

16 Stent GS (1977) *Paradoxes of Progress.* Freeman, CA.

17 Sir Roger Penrose FRS, Professor of Mathematics at Oxford University and author of *The Emperor's New Mind* and *Shadows of the Mind*, was the 1999 Gresham Professor of Geometry and the other mathematical sciences, giving two free public lectures (in a continuous series of Gresham College lectures going back 400 years, with only a brief interruption for World War Two), which I attended near the beginning of my sabbatical.

18 *Class Talk* by Colin Hannaford, Director of the Institute for Democracy through Mathematics, Oxford (*New Scientist*, 28 August 1999). The point of this article is that instead of using mathematics and logic as democratising forces, as the ancient Greeks intended, modern education is subverting them to the imprisonment of young minds.

19 *Composed upon Westminster Bridge*, by William Wordsworth.

20 Dawkins R (1986) *The Blind Watchmaker.* Longman, Harlow. My favourite description (of many that Dawkins has written) is the wonderful account of a bat flying by echolocation in *The Blind Watchmaker* (p. 24, hardback edition): 'These bats are like miniature spy planes, bristling with sophisticated instrumentation . . .'

21 Feynman RP (a Nobel prize-winner in physics) (1985) *'Surely You're Joking, Mr Feynman.' Adventures of a Curious Character.* Bantam Press, London.

22   de Bono E (1970) *Lateral Thinking: a Textbook of Creativity.* Penguin, London.

23   Kipling R (1910) The way through the woods. In: *Rewards and Fairies.* Wordsworth Collection Childrens Library (1999).

24   Schrödinger's classic thought experiment has a cat concealed in a box containing a device which will release a poisonous gas if and when it is triggered by some chance quantum event such as the decay of an atom in a radioactive isotope. Quantum mechanics holds, indeed it is the new orthodoxy, that the cat is both alive *and* dead until the box is opened and the matter is resolved by the fact of being observed.

25   Adams S (1997) *Dogbert's Top Secret Management Guide.* Boxtree, London.

26   Benner P (1984) *From Novice to Expert: Excellence and Power in Clinical Nursing Practice.* Addison-Wesley Publishing Co., Menlo Park, CA.

27   Dreyfus HL and Dreyfus SE (1977) *Uses and Abuses of Multi-Attribute and Multi-Aspect Models of Decision-Making,* Unpublished manuscript. Department of Industrial Engineering and Operations Research, University of California at Berkeley (this is the reference as quoted by Patricia Benner).

28   Stent GS (1977) *Paradoxes of Progress.* Freeman, CA. A collection of 11 essays written between 1969 and 1977.

29   Frayn M (1998) *Copenhagen.* Methuen, London.

30   Bonn D and Bonn J (2000) Work-related stress: can it be a thing of the past? *Lancet.* **8 January**: 355.

31   Borneo is 12 000 km from Britain. If the television screen is 3 metres away, then the scene in Borneo is $12\,000 \times 1000/3$ times as far away – a magnification of 4 million.

32   The *Winfract* program which accompanies the book, Wegner T, Peterson M, Tyler B and Branderhorst P (1992) *Fractals for Windows.* The Waite Group, Corte Madera, CA. This book is now out of print but the program Fractint can be downloaded from the Fractint homepage.

33   The *Concise Oxford Dictionary* states that the saying 'many a mickle makes a muckle', although original, was erroneous because a mickle and a muckle *both* used to mean a large amount. It prefers the form 'many a little makes a mickle', which seems rather pedantic, but the modern English version it offers is clear enough: 'many small amounts accumulate to make a large amount'.

34   'There are about 800 million publicly available web pages on the Web, but even the best search engines index only 16% of them. Two years ago, the best search engines indexed a third of the 320 million pages that were on the web.' (This Week, *New Scientist*, 10 July 1999).

35   Pirsig RM (1991) *LILA: an Inquiry into Morals.* Bantam, London.

36   This thought prevented me taking a sabbatical for years – I thought that the front-line view I was trying to articulate could only be expressed

from the heat of the battle (as was my first book). I hope that I have reached a reasonable compromise, but perhaps this is the place to state that everything has been reviewed, checked for validity, much reorganised and much rewritten during the subsequent 12 months, with me back and refreshed at work.

37   This fairly obvious neologism was original when I thought of it, but I have seen it used independently in an article since.

38   Diogenes (400–325 BC), Greek cynic philosopher who lived a life of extreme austerity inside a barrel. He is remembered for his reply 'Get out of my light' when Alexander the Great asked him whether there was anything he could do for him. It is generally accepted that the term 'Diogenes syndrome' is a misnomer, representing as it does the opposite pole of acquisitiveness from Diogenes himself, but the name has nonetheless become established in popular usage.

39   Winston Churchill's speech to the House of Commons: '. . . the battle of France is over. I expect that the Battle of Britain is about to begin. On this battle depends the survival of Christian civilisation . . .' *Hansard*, 18 June 1940, column 40.

40   Charon (in Greek myth), the ferryman who brought the dead across the river Styx or Acheron to Hades.

41   Ackroyd P (1995) *Blake*. Minerva, London.

42   This happened on 20 July 2000.

43   Lempert T, Gresty A and Bronstein AM (1995) Benign positional vertigo: recognition and treatment. *BMJ*. **311**: 489–91. (Figure 3 was printed in mirror image and subsequently amended.)

44   *As You Like It*, Act 2, Scene 7.

45   The Gospel according to St Matthew, Ch 6, v 24.

46   It is a Cornish and Breton legend that Troy was re-founded by Brutus on the site of what is now Fowey.

47   Peter Greens writes in his biography of Kenneth Grahame (*Beyond the Wild Woods*) that '. . . the Purves brothers confirm that the opening chapter "The River Bank" was inspired by a boating trip up the Fowey River, undertaken by Grahame, Atky and their father . . .'

48   Gladwell M (2000) *The Tipping Point*. Little, Brown & Co., London.

49   Callil C and Toibin C (eds) (1999) *The Modern Library: the 200 Best Novels in English Since 1950*. Picador, London.

50   The large body of meticulous research and statistical analysis of the monk Gregor Mendel was the foundation of the science of genetics. Although it was published in 1866, the work lay unnoticed until three separate workers rediscovered it more or less independently in 1900, Mendel himself having died in 1884. Even then it was not until the 1920s and 1930s that its revolutionary significance for evolution was appreciated. *Encarta*.

51 See my discussion of this in *The Paradox of Progress*, Chapter 2, 'Our distorted view of the world' (published in 1995 by Radcliffe Medical Press, Oxford).

52 See my own website at friendsinlowplaces.co.uk

53 Buzzword bingo has been variously attributed, but I first saw it described in one of Miles Kington's columns in *The Independent*. Each time a speaker at a meeting uses a buzzword, players pick up their pencils and mark their cards, giving an appreciative smile and nod. When they complete a line on the card they may punch the air or make other demonstrations of enthusiasm. The speaker is delighted by the constant appreciative feedback, and the listeners get credit for attentiveness and being abreast of the in-house jargon.

54 Council houses were built by local authorities for rent to local, mainly working people.

55 'Meals-on-wheels' are subsidised meals distributed by volunteers to disabled people in their homes.

56 ISQ: *in status quo* – shorthand commonly used in medical notes to mean 'condition unchanged'.

57 See *The Paradox of Progress*, Chapter 2.

58 Greenhalgh T and Hurwitz B (eds) (1998) *Narrative-Based Medicine: Dialogue and Discourse in Clinical Practice*. BMJ Books, London.

59 Willis JAR (1986) Simple scale for assessing level of dependency of patients in general practice. *BMJ.* **292**: 1639–40; Willis JAR (1986) Bringing the visiting diary up to date. *BMJ.* **292**: 1715–16.

60 Schooler J and Engstler-Schooler T (1990) Verbal overshadowing of visual memories: some things are better left unsaid. *Cogn Psychol.* **22**: 36–71; Schooler J, Ohlsoson S and Brooks K (1993) Thought beyond words: when language overshadows sight. *J Exp Psychol.* **122**: 166–83; Schooler J and Melcher J (1995) The ineffability of insight. In: SM Smith *et al.* (eds) *The Creative Cognition Approach*. Publishing House.

61 Claxton G (1998) *Hare Brain Tortoise Mind: Why Intelligence Increases as You Think Less*. Fourth Estate, London.

62 'The process is not that of photographing individual facts, but the far more sophisticated and useful one of fine-tuning a personal synthesis. The fact that doctors, amongst others, do manage this process into the teeth of the head wind of contemporary educational effort suggests how very much better they would be able to do it if only contemporary education recognised this fact and exerted its undoubted energy on finding ways of enhancing rather than hindering it.' *The Paradox of Progress*, p. 81.

63 Dawkins R (1996) *Climbing Mount Improbable*. Viking, London. Dawkins represents evolution as the process of climbing a mountain which has subsidiary peaks arising from its slopes. When evolution carries a

species up a subsidiary peak, there may be such a disadvantage to coming down again to rejoin the route up the main mountain that the species gets stuck there, like the horseshoe crab or the coelacanth (or the IBM personal computer), unable to develop any further towards what would have been a more advanced state which would have been accessible if it had taken a different route lower down.

64 Jonscher C (1999) *Wired Life.* Transworld Publishers, London.

65 Hodges A (1997) *Alan Turing: a Natural Philosopher.* Phoenix, London.

66 Nuclear fusion is the power released when two small atoms (e.g. of hydrogen) combine to form a single larger atom. It is many orders of magnitude larger than the power of nuclear fission, which is released when a large, relatively unstable atom such as uranium is split into two smaller atoms. Nuclear fission is the power of nuclear reactors and of the atomic bombs which destroyed Hiroshima and Nagasaki at the end of the Second World War. Hydrogen bombs are made by exploding an atomic bomb inside a jacket of hydrogen. They have never been used except in tests. As a source of peace-time energy, nuclear fusion holds enormous potential, as the hydrogen fuel is effectively infinite, and the process should not produce radioactivity. However, concerted international research has all but abandoned hope of finding a safe way of subjecting hydrogen to the enormous temperatures and pressures required for fusion.

67 Jonscher gives 20 billion (20 000 million) as the figure for the number of neurones in the brain throughout his book. The figure which is more usually quoted is 100 billion, which is memorable because it also happens to be the number of stars in a galaxy and the number of galaxies in the universe. All of these figures are, of course, approximations, and whichever one of them is more nearly 'right' doesn't make any difference to the points being made.

68 Sennett R (1998) *The Corrosion of Character: the Personal Consequences of Work in the New Capitalism.* WW Norton, New York.

69 Greaves D (1996) *Mystery in Western Medicine.* Avebury, Aldershot.

70 Pirsig RM (1988) *Zen and the Art of Motorcycle Maintenance.* Vintage, London (first published in the UK by Bodley Head in 1974).

71 Capra F (1992) *The Tao of Physics: an Exploration of the Parallels Between Modern Physics and Eastern Mysticism* (3e). Flamingo, London (first published by Fontana in 1976).

72 Toffler A (1980) *The Third Wave.* William Collins Sons & Co. Ltd, London.

73 Heath I (1995) *The Mystery of General Practice.* John Fry Trust Fellowship, The Nuffield Provincial Hospitals Trust.

74 Skrabanek P and McCormick J (1992) *Follies and Fallacies in Medicine* (2e). The Tarragon Press, London (first edition published in 1989).

75   Skrabanek P (1994) *The Death of Human Medicine and the Rise of Coercive Healthism*. The Social Affairs Unit, London.

76   Sweeney B (1998) The place of the humanities in the education of a doctor. The 1997 James Mackenzie Lecture. *Br J Gen Pract*. **February**: 998–1002.

77   Evans M and Sweeney K (1998) *The Human Side of Medicine*. Occasional Paper 76. Royal College of General Practitioners, London.

78   Le Fanu J (2000) *The Rise and Fall of Western Medicine*. Abacus, London.

79   The drug thalidomide was introduced in 1957 as an exceptionally safe treatment for morning sickness of pregnancy, which meant that it was given during the crucial early stage of development of the fetus. In 1961, there were simultaneous reports from Sydney, Australia and Hamburg (West Germany) of newborn babies suffering from phocomelia – seal-limb – a hitherto extremely rare deformity in which the arms and/or legs were not properly formed. In West Germany alone there were some 10 000 cases, of whom 5000 survived, and in Britain there were 600 cases, of whom 400 survived. The drug-licensing authorities in the USA delayed the approval of thalidomide, so the USA suffered very few cases. The drug was withdrawn from use worldwide in 1962.

80   Thematic Issue (1999) Advancing the evidence-based healthcare debate. *J Eval Clin Pract*. **5**(2).

81   Postcards from the Fens (1999) *Br J Gen Pract*. **May**: 412–13. Quotes respectively from the conference reports by David Haslam, Tina Ambury and Joe Neary.

82   Wessex has not been a recognised geographical area since the Middle Ages, but it is used by the Royal College of General Practitioners as the name of one of its 25 faculties. The Wessex faculty extends across a large tract of southern England, from Alton in the east to Bath in the west, and includes the Isle of Wight.

83   Dr Ivan Kopell. My thanks to him.

84   Cyclosporin is the drug which suppresses the body's immune reaction to transplanted tissue (which, unless it is from an identical twin, would otherwise be recognised as foreign and rejected by the body, however closely matched the donor). Transplant recipients must take it, or similar successor drugs, for the rest of their lives. It has made organ transplantation possible.

85   It is a remarkable fact that of all the media, the theatre has done most to clarify the concepts of contemporary physics for the general mind. Michael Frayn's *Copenhagen* follows Tom Stoppard's plays *Jumpers* and *Hapgood* in this respect.

86   Gribbin J (1984) *In Search of Schrödinger's Cat*. Corgi, London.

87   Goodwin JS (1997) Chaos and the limits of modern medicine. *JAMA*. **278**: 1400 (as quoted by Iona Heath).

88 Magee B (1973) *Popper*. Fontana, London.

89 Willis J (1999) Rules can never describe life, they can only set limits. *Br J Gen Pract.* **April:** 330–1.

90 Dr Harold Shipman, the notorious multiple murderer, was well known for complying with performance indicators. He was in many ways a respected doctor, whom I heard lecturing on the use of computers in practice barely 18 months before his final arrest. An earlier investigation by the police had failed to find any evidence upon which to act, *even though they knew what they were looking for.* Yet this case has led directly to routine checks on all doctors with the explicit aim of reassuring the public that a similar case can never happen again.

91 'Doctors who fail new checks to be struck off', *Guardian* headline, 2 February 1999.

92 Charlton BG (1999) The ideology of accountability. *J R Coll Phys Lond.* **33:** 33–5.

93 Two schools in the same town may well be inseparable in terms of league-table results, while local people have a sophisticated and detailed knowledge of the differences between them. The irresistible impression that league-tables are more valid and more fair than this kind of informal 'local knowledge' is a spurious side-effect of the dominance of the fixed and the absolute in human perceptions.

94 Russell A (1972) 'How to write your own Gilbert and Sullivan opera'. From *Anna Russell: the Anna Russell Album*. Sony, London.

95 Popper K (1945) *The Open Society and Its Enemies*. Routledge & Kegan Paul, London.

96 The hypothetical question of whether rules on when to think a thought would follow if a technology to 'read' thoughts were to emerge is interesting, in view of the uses to which we have put information technology (the sudden emergence of which was entirely unforeseen, even by George Orwell). Surely there would be a strong pressure for the creation of such rules, which might prove impossible to resist. They could easily be presented as an 'inevitable' part of 'progress'.

97 Standard Attainment Tasks.

98 Americans could never understand this when they assumed that 'socialised medicine' meant communist-style central direction. Ironically, it was only under the avowedly freedom-loving Conservative government of Margaret Thatcher that central direction was introduced in her so-called 'reforms' which were imposed, against the will of the medical profession and of the public, in 1990.

99 *Easter 1916*, by WB Yeats: '… All changed, changed utterly: a terrible beauty is born.'

100 Smith R (1998) All changed, changed utterly (editorial). *BMJ.* **316:** 1917–18. http://www.bmj.com/cgi/content/full/316/7149/1917

101 Anomalies I have found while using Series 5 READ codes under the EMIS practice computer system:

Duplicate codes

Prostatism	1AA
Prostatism	K20-6

i.e. if one doctor chooses 1AA to code patients with prostatism (symptoms of enlargement of the prostate gland) and another chooses K20-6, subsequent comparisons may produce spurious differences between their two experiences.

Viral illness	EGTON290
Viral illness	A79z-1
Hormone replacement therapy	8B64
Hormone replacement therapy	66U-1
Perianal haematoma	G844-1
Perianal haematoma	SE231-1
Finger sprain	S5210-1
Sprain finger	S523
Acute tonsillitis	H03
Acute Tonsilitis	H03-97

i.e. the only apparent differences between these last two codes are the spelling and capitalisation.

Tired all the time	1683
Tired all the time	E205-2
Toothache	1912
Toothache	J05y-1
Seborrhoeic wart	M221-1
Seborrhoeic wart	M22C
Seborrhoeic wart	M22-z-2
Nocturia	1A13
Nocturia	R0842
Juvenile plantar dermatosis*	M1B
Juvenile plantar dermatitis*	M1B-1
Juvenile plantar dermatosis**	M2y48
Juvenile plantar dermatitis**	M2y48-1

  * These are alternative names for the same thing.
** These are simple duplicates of the preceding pair.

102   The Comte de Charolais (the brother of one of the Marquis de Sade's father's mistresses) 'exemplified all the most bloodthirsty traits of his age and class, shooting peasants for sport and taking pot-shots at workmen repairing roofs in a neighbouring village'. The abuse of power in eighteenth-century Ancien Régime French society was taking place barely 200 years ago, among people who we regard as having been in other respects supremely civilised. (Source: Review by Michael Arditti of two new books on de Sade in *The Independent Weekend Review*, 10 July 1999.)

103   Ionesco E (1960) *Rhinoceros*. Ionesco Plays, Vol 4. John Calder, London. First produced in Paris by Jean-Louis Barrault at the Odéon on 25 January 1960.

104   Cameron J (1995) *The Artist's Way: a Course in Discovering and Recovering Your Creative Self*. Pan, London.

105   This is an exact transcript of the closing moments of a tape recording which I hold of Radio Four's *Call You and Yours* phone-in debate from early 1999, featuring Polly Toynbee, journalist and distinguished social commentator, and Ian Walker, a spokesman for the legal profession. The subject was the rights and wrongs of medical litigation.

106   I am estimating that there are about 146 000 working days in 400 years.

107   The author was one of two GP members of the Caldicott Committee enquiry into the confidentiality of medical records.

108   I once had a patient who needed a particular drug in pregnancy, but the manufacturer's advice said that it was contraindicated. It was the best drug for the purpose, so I telephoned the manufacturer's medical advice department. They did a search of their records and found that the warning resulted from a single incident of a relatively minor effect reported in one pregnancy, out of millions of patients treated, with no indication that it was related to the drug at all. I explained the situation and my patient took the drug without trouble.

109   Willis JAR (1999) The pen is mightier than the scalpel. *J Eval Clin Med*. **August**: 343–6.

110   Mithin S (1996) *The Prehistory of the Mind: a Search for the Origins of Art, Religion and Science*. Phoenix/Thames and Hudson, London.

111   'I have only one eye . . . I have a right to be blind sometimes . . . I really do not see the signal' (Horatio Nelson at the Battle of Copenhagen, 1801). Quoted in Southey R (1813) *Life of Nelson*, Chapter 7. Second in command to Sir Hyde Parker, Nelson ignored his signal to withdraw and led the whole fleet in an attack which destroyed the Danish fleet in its harbour. He was given the title of Viscount Lord Nelson shortly afterwards. (This story has, I believe, something useful to say about authority.)

112 Patients who used to buy their own paracetamol now very reasonably ask for a prescription because local shops are currently charging 99p for the new packs of 14 tablets.

113 Horden J (1998) *The End of Science*. Abacus, London.

114 Fukuyama F (1993) *The End of History and the Last Man*. Penguin, Harmondsworth.

115 Goodman NW (1998) Clinical governance. *BMJ*. **317**: 1725–7.

116 *The Pursuit of the Ideal*, by Isaiah Berlin (1909–1997). Quoted in the obituary by Bernard Crick, *Guardian*, 7 November 1997.

117 The end of the twentieth century has seen reports of unsatisfactory military equipment, large proportions of the RAF's fighter force not being airworthy, and enormously expensive computer projects failing.

118 Doing a jigsaw puzzle: you decide on a system, you collect all of the red pieces and your friend collects all of the blue pieces. This is very efficient until you find pieces with both colours. Life is a jigsaw puzzle with four dimensions, an infinity of pieces, an infinity of solutions and an irresistible illusion that one of them is best.

119 Turing AM (1950) Computing machinery and intelligence. *Mind*. **59**: 433. Reprinted in Hofstadter DR and Dennet DC (eds) (1981) *The Mind's I*. Basic Books Inc., Harmondsworth.

120 The infective larva of the parasitic worm *Toxocara canis* is an intestinal parasite of dogs which can infect humans. The remote danger that it can cause blindness (almost never in both eyes) has resulted in disproportionate stigmatisation of dogs as pets.

121 For many years, Alton Abbey provided accommodation for vagrant men. New accommodation standards were then introduced, forcing closure and returning some of the inmates to homelessness.

122 Associate Professor of Family Medicine and Paediatrics at McGill University, Montreal, speaking at the *Primary Care 92* conference at the Wembley Conference Centre, London.

123 Rudy Giuliani presided over a 70% reduction in violent crime and murder rates in New York City. Thought by many to have taken authoritarianism too far (jailing Mafia bosses and getting intimidating squeegee-men off the city's road junctions was fine – prosecuting jaywalkers and driving hot-dog vendors off the streets was perhaps less so), and to have given too little credit to others who helped him, but his achievements are undeniable. (Source: Profile by David Usborne, *The Independent Weekend Review*, 10 July 1999.)

124 'Traditional GP "must adapt" to new NHS. The "traditional" GP has no choice but to adapt to the rush of changes in the health service, the conference heard ... representatives warmed to the sentiments of Dr Michael Bosch from Surrey, who said "I love working as a GP. I think I have the best job in the world. That will be the key to

having enough young people in the future – to be as keen as I am."' Report on the 1999 Conference of Local Medical Committees (*Doctor*, 1 July 1999).

125 Bryson B (1990) *Mother Tongue: the English Language*. Penguin, Harmondsworth.

126 Paterson D (ed) (1999) *101 Sonnets: from Shakespeare to Heaney*. Faber and Faber, London.

127 A syringe-driver is a battery-powered device that administers a continuous injection of painkilling and/or sedative drugs via a tiny needle that lies unobtrusively in the wall of the abdomen. It is set up for a whole day at a time and avoids disturbing dying patients and their relatives with the often difficult job of giving drugs by mouth. It also allows pain control to be continuous, and has proved to be an invaluable aid in the care of patients who are dying in their own homes.

128 Department of Health (2000) *The NHS Plan: a Plan for Investment, a Plan for Reform*. The Stationery Office, London.

129 *The NHS Plan*, para 1.22.

130 Letter to the General Assembly of the Kirk of Scotland, 3 August 1650, in Thomas Carlyle (1845) *Oliver Cromwell's Letters and Speeches*.

131 *Middlemarch* by George Eliot. Book 2, Chapter 20 (1985 edition). Penguin Classics, Harmondsworth.

132 Junger S (1997) *The Perfect Storm*. Fourth Estate, London.

133 Havel V (1991) The power of the powerless. In: *Open Letters*. Faber and Faber, London.

134 Hillary R (1942) *The Last Enemy*. Pimlico, London. This work recounts Richard Hillary's experiences as a fighter pilot in World War Two, in which he was shot down and spent months in hospital undergoing operations to rebuild his face and hands. It was first published in 1942, seven months before his death in a second crash.

135 Speaking to groups of doctors at academic meetings around the turn of the millennium, I find a confident belief that my fears concerning the abuse of hard science in medicine are exaggerated, although my observations about the current difficulties in practising medicine are almost universally accepted.

136 Rules for rules, in *The Paradox of Progress*, p. 123.

137 A GP is a self-contained, mobile, information-gathering device equipped to detect light, sound, temperature, texture, movement, scent and mood with greater sensitivity than any machine, and with a unique and little understood ability to collate that information into a coherent picture which it relates to a broad background model of the world, the universe and everything – including, in particular, a working representation of the corpus of medical knowledge.

Index